ALSO FROM THE AUTHOR:

The Almanack of Naval Ravikant: A Guide to Wealth and Happiness

The Anthology of Balaji: A Guide to Technology, Truth, and Building the Future

THE BOOK OF ELON

A GUIDE TO PURPOSE AND SUCCESS
Elon Musk's Most Useful Ideas,
in His Own Words

THE
BOOK
OF
ELON

Foreword by
NAVAL RAVIKANT

ERIC JORGENSON
Visuals by **JACK BUTCHER**

COPYRIGHT © 2026 ERIC JORGENSON
All rights reserved.

THE BOOK OF ELON
A Guide to Purpose and Success

FIRST EDITION

ISBN 978-1-5445-5075-6 *Hardcover*
         978-1-5445-5074-9 *Paperback*
         978-1-5445-5076-3 *Ebook*

FOR MY PROGENY...

THE REASON I DO (ALMOST) EVERYTHING.

CONTENTS

NOTES ON THIS BOOK	15
FOREWORD	17
ERIC'S WELCOME TO THIS BOOK	21

PART I: PURSUE PURPOSE

LIVING A PURPOSEFUL LIFE	31
Be Useful	32
Fight for the Future	35
Obsess for Success	38
Start Before the World Is Ready	40
Create More than You Consume	41
Work like Hell	44
Feel the Fear; Do It Anyway	47
Seek the Nature of the Universe	49
THINK LIKE A PHYSICIST	53
Obsess over Truth	54
First-Principles Thinking	58
Thinking in Limits	63
Aspire to Be Less Wrong	68
THE VALUE OF ENGINEERING	73
Engineering Is Magic	74
Engineering Wins Wars	77
Engineering Creates Value	81

PART II: ULTRA HARDCORE WORK

WHAT IT TAKES — 85
- Take Responsibility — 86
- Earn Deep Understanding — 88
- Sleep on the Factory Floor — 90
- Frontline Leadership — 91
- Adversity Forges Strength — 93
- Eat Glass and Stare into the Abyss — 96

BUILDING EXCEPTIONAL TEAMS — 99
- A Group with a Goal — 100
- Create a Culture of Builders — 102
- Recruit for Exceptional Ability — 105
- Retain Only Special Forces — 107
- Feedback over Feelings — 109

DESIGNING THE ORGANIZATION — 111
- Remove Organizational Boundaries — 112
- Simple Communication — 117
- Innovation Needs Permission to Fail — 119
- Simplicity Wins — 124
- The Algorithm — 130

MANIACAL URGENCY — 139
- Don't Waste Time — 140
- Speed Is Both Offense and Defense — 141
- Do Things in Parallel — 143
- Break Down the "Impossible" — 146
- Set Aggressive Timelines — 148

WE MUST MAKE STUFF — 151
- The Real Work — 152
- The Factory Is the Product — 154
- Attack the Constraint — 156
- Manufacturing Is the Moat — 158

PART III: BUILDING COMPANIES

BECOMING A FOUNDER — 163
- Starting Zip2 — 168
- Going All In, Again (Zip2 Earnings into PayPal) — 173
- Listen Well, Correct Fast — 176
- Unite and Conquer — 181
- From Exile to Exit — 184

BUILDING TESLA — 187
- The Mission to Protect the Planet — 188
- Going All In, Again (PayPal Earnings into Tesla) — 192
- Building the First Prototype — 193
- Becoming Tesla's CEO — 197
- Sequenced Strategy of Tesla — 199
- Keeping Tesla Alive — 202
- The Edge of Sanity — 205
- A Whole New Kind of Car Company — 207
- Give People More for Less — 211
- The Battle of Public Perception — 214
- Founding SolarCity — 216

BUILDING SPACEX — 219
- The Only One Crazy Enough for Space — 220
- I Expected to Lose Everything — 222
- Rockets from First Principles — 228
- Keeping SpaceX Alive — 231
- Landing NASA Contracts — 234
- You Have to Blow Things Up — 236
- Building the Just Barely Possible — 240
- Optimizing for Mass to Mars — 246

PART IV: ON BEHALF OF HUMANITY

BUILDING OUR FUTURE — 251
- Companies Are Philanthropy — 252
- Companies Create Wealth for All — 254
- Companies to Start — 258
- Companies Drive Progress — 262

THE AGE OF ABUNDANCE — 265
- The End of Scarcity — 266
- Exponential Intelligence — 268
- Upgrading the Human Mind — 269
- The Last Human Drivers — 276
- Sustainable Abundance — 280

OUR EXISTENTIAL RISKS — 283
- This Is the Best Time to Be Alive — 284
- World War III — 287
- Regulation Accumulation — 290
- Unsustainable Energy — 294
- Misaligned Artificial Superintelligence — 297
- Population Collapse — 304
- Asteroids and Comets — 310

BECOMING MULTIPLANETARY — 311
- Becoming Multiplanetary Is an Evolutionary-Scale Event — 312
- If You Love Life, Protect It — 316
- The Gateway to Mars — 318
- Building the New World — 323
- Colonizing the Galaxy — 329

BONUS

THE **69** CORE MUSK METHODS	335
TIMELINE OF ELON MUSK	339
ELON'S RECOMMENDED READING	343
WANT MORE?	355
APPRECIATION	357
ABOUT THE AUTHOR	361
SOURCES	363

NOTES ON THIS BOOK

This is a book of Elon's ideas in his own words. I built this book entirely out of transcripts, tweets, and interviews over his entire life to date. The body of this book comes directly from him. On this, a few important points:

→ Transcripts have been edited for clarity, brevity, and flow multiple times.
→ Given potential for fakes, edits, and misquotes, I can't be certain of every source's authenticity.
→ Please verify phrasing with a primary source before citing Elon from this book.
→ Please interpret generously.

Everything in this book is taken out of context. To create this book, I recontextualized ideas in an attempt to make them more accessible, useful, and memorable.

As ideas passed through time, space, and medium, phrasing may have shifted in flight. Every effort was made to keep the original intent, but errors are possible. His original intent may be different from your interpretation in a different time, format, and context.

All brilliance in this book is Elon's; any mistakes are mine.

HIGHLIGHTS

Highlights are used to summarize or punctuate an idea. You could flip through the book reading just these and find valuable ideas. Highlights are easy to spot because they look like this:

> I am a highlight.

BOLDED QUESTIONS

Many excerpts are from interviews; some are written to provide proper context. The questions help create the feeling of an intimate dialogue between you and Elon.

SKIP AROUND

Jump to anything that interests you and skip anything that doesn't. This is a choose-your-own-adventure book, though some ideas build on previous examples.

FOREWORD

— BY NAVAL RAVIKANT

You're holding in your hands the only book an entrepreneur needs. A lone founder takes a unique journey to discover and encapsulate the truth into a product. Weighted by responsibility and expectation, the founder seeks out mentors and books—but the best mentors can't be hired, and the books are either anecdotal or academic. The only reliable teacher is bitter experience.

In this book, Eric put his ego aside and did the thankless work of compiling Elon's best lessons, in Elon's own words, as practical as possible. This isn't a tedious biography or recounting of events, it's the explanation and the manual. An eager co-founder stole my first copy, and my coworkers will get the next twenty.

Elon is the greatest entrepreneur since Steve Jobs, but he isn't just a copy. History doesn't repeat, but it does rhyme, and it's the occasional Napoleon, whether in science, art, or politics, who appears and reroutes the inexorable forces of history with a unique vision and drive. Hard work is common, intelligence uncommon, courage rare—and Elon combusts all three.

The banal observation is that he's a founder of Tesla, SpaceX, OpenAI, and Neuralink. These companies, however, are just means to products—the self-driving cars, the autonomous robots, the thinking machines, and the awe-inspiring, ground-shattering, heavy rockets that thunder into space and land on their toes. Even the products are just a means unto the mission. If it's allowed by the laws of physics, and takes us into our sci-fi dreams, Elon will drag us there.

The wealth, the fame, and the envy are a byproduct. Crabs in the gravity well, blinded by politics, will point to his father's and the government's money. But envy says more about the envious than the envied. Elon sleeps on the factory floor, doubles down every time, and never gives up. The people worth impressing are impressed, and millions of children are inspired to make real change. Culture is downstream of the technology that enables us to be generous and free, and Elon will be remembered long after the big talkers and small doers are forgotten.

As Chief Engineer, Elon reminds us that building value is building things, not financing or managing them. It's a better world when the richest man is one who creates wealth, rather than shuffles it around, or seizes it in the name of the people.

Wealth, as the physicist David Deutsch wrote, is the set of physical transformations that we can effect—true for both individuals and societies. The main component of wealth is knowledge, not capital. By creating new knowledge, and then instantiating it in products that are duplicated and distributed, Elon and his fellow entrepreneurs are engines of wealth creation and distribution.

You may have the opportunity to ask yourself: When humanity went to the stars, what were you doing? When men walked on Mars, were you mocking them or exhorting them? When they mined the first asteroids and built the first space stations? When fleets of self-driving cars reclaimed cities from parking and traffic? When the paraplegics rose up and walked alongside us? When the robots took over the miserable and repetitive work? Were you in the front row, cheering? Or sour-faced in the bleachers, jeering?

There is even a third option—young or old, your life isn't over yet. Elon's methods are copy-able, in matters big and small. Eric has laid them out for you as plainly as possible. If your motives are pure and greater than yourself, the world will conspire in its subtle ways to help you. When one man shows what's possible, a million arise, not as followers, but as missionaries in their own right.

You don't have to do what Elon does, and you don't have to do it his way, but this short life is best spent in the arena, on something other than the mundane and insatiable self. Reject the craving for comfort and social approval. Reorient to the optimism of youth. Leave those talking and dividing, and get on the path to learning and building.

Your energy is best spent with like-minded people who are unstoppable on a mission to make something beautiful. Don't make the thing to make the money, make the money so that you can make the thing. Don't get paid for work, get paid so that you can do your best work. Rise up, choose inspiration over envy, and show your younger and older selves that the desires of this life were completely and totally exhausted into the universal will.

ERIC'S WELCOME TO THIS BOOK

Hello, and welcome!

I'm delighted you picked up this book. I've put thousands of hours into collecting, curating, and editing Elon's most useful ideas for you.

You may be seeking purpose, a mission worthy of your life's effort. You might already have a clear purpose and seek the tools for success. You will find both in this book.

Elon's purpose is to help humanity survive and thrive. He thinks in sweeping timescales, like a sci-fi epic. By funding and leading SpaceX and Tesla, Elon Musk has done the entrepreneurial equivalent of running a two-minute mile. Twice. *At the same time*.

Regardless of your industry, mission, or beliefs—there is something to learn from this feat.

After seeing what Elon and his teams have accomplished, we stand taller, and the universe seems smaller.

To me, Musk represents the idea that I am capable of more than I ever imagined. Even more importantly, he shows that together we are capable of the currently impossible.

He models our moral duty to grab the impossible and drag it into the possible through massive effort, ingenuity, and force of will. This is how we build an ever-better future.

In the past, the richest man on Earth was a monarch, oil heir, or financier. Now, the richest man on Earth is an engineer, entrepreneur, and American immigrant who has taken massive personal risks to build new things that solve problems on a planetary—and interplanetary—scale. We are learning to respect the builders more than the rulers.

Elon Musk has joined a lineage of legendary entrepreneurs who transformed our culture. Henry Ford's greatest impact was creating car culture. Steve Jobs's greatest impact was on computer culture. Elon Musk's greatest impact will be advancing the culture of engineering, entrepreneurship, and adventure over the next century.

Elon's energy, vision, and his team's achievements have stoked a fire in my chest. I feel *activated* to advance human prosperity, knowing that humans are a few years into an inspiring million-year journey of knowledge and construction. Working on this book gave me a new level of spiritual satisfaction and inspiration. You and I may be ants, but we are building an intergalactic cathedral.

I want you to stare down the biggest problems humanity faces and attack them with furious ingenuity. If the next generation has one million Musks, our grandchildren will flourish beyond our wildest dreams.

One million Musks. That's my dream for this book.

Seeing life-changing ideas dissolve into the algorithms breaks my heart. I build these books to rescue knowledge and preserve it in our most proven, permanent format.

When I create books, I focus on making them as useful as possible. No fluff, no filler. I hope you have a highlight on every single page.

As you read, imagine you are out to dinner with Elon Musk. You're deep in conversation as he shares stories and ideas you can apply in your own life and work. I hope you feel personally tutored by the greatest living entrepreneur.

I focus entirely on Elon's most useful ideas. We spend zero pages on Elon's family life or politics. This is not a biography or a gossip column. My books are about sharing timeless ideas that work.

This book has four parts:

1. **Pursue Purpose:** The foundations of a unique life
2. **Ultra Hardcore Work:** Mindsets and principles for achieving the barely possible
3. **Building Companies:** Stories and strategies from PayPal, Tesla, and SpaceX
4. **On Behalf of Humanity:** How you can be part of elevating the future of humanity

The first half is filled with principles and tactics Elon uses to guide his life and build his companies. I guarantee you will get valuable ideas in the first few pages.

The second half has more stories. They share Elon's adventures and how he applied his principles to choose worthy missions and built SpaceX and Tesla. We finish with Elon's view of the years ahead and how you can make an impact.

When you're done reading (maybe a few times!), I hope you enact more of Elon's hardcore work ethic, boundless optimism, and unabashed courage.

If this book resonates with you, know that we're fast friends. You're joining a global community of allies in pushing progress. I'd love to hear from you and hope you will help us spread these ideas far and wide. Let's leave humanity better than we found it.

Forward. Together.

Eric

*"All of physics is either impossible or trivial.
It is impossible until you understand
it, and then it becomes trivial."*

—ERNEST RUTHERFORD[1]

Now, here is Elon in his own words...

PART I

PURSUE
PURPOSE

> I don't mind if my legacy is accurate or inaccurate, as long as I die feeling I've done the right thing for the future of Consciousness.[2]

LIVING A PURPOSEFUL LIFE

You can choose to be not ordinary.

You can choose not to conform to the conventions taught by your parents.

It's possible for ordinary people to choose to be extraordinary.[3]

BE USEFUL

Don't aspire to glory; aspire to work.[4]

The measure of success in my life is: "How many useful things can I get done?"

On a day-to-day basis, I wake up in the morning and ask, "How can I be useful today?"

I want to maximize my utility. It's difficult to be useful at scale.[5]

I can't always get it right, but I aspire to make our future good. Sometimes I make mistakes. But, I try to take the set of actions most likely to improve the probability that the future will be good.[6]

Try to be useful. Do useful things for your fellow human beings and the world. It's hard to be useful, to contribute more than you consume. Can you have a positive net contribution to society? Aim for that.[7]

I have a lot of respect for someone who puts in an honest day's work to do useful things. I admire anyone making a positive contribution to humanity. Whether that is in farming, technology, entertainment, or whatever else. To anyone useful to the rest of humanity: I admire you greatly.[8]

Q: How do you know if you're helping?

I think about it mathematically. How many people you helped, multiplied by how much help you provided each person, on average. How many people you helped, and how much—that's the total utility (usefulness).[9] It's almost like the physics definition of true work. If you aspire to do true work, your probability of success is much higher.[10]

For any product you're trying to create, ask yourself the utility improvement compared to the current state of the art, multiplied by how many people it would affect.

Building something that makes a big difference to a small number of people is just as great as something that makes a small difference for a vast number of people. Mathematically, the total positive impact would be roughly similar for those two things. It's about trying to be useful.[11]

This is the mathematical first principles perspective—utility and numbers. Is some simple app really making people's lives better? If it's affecting a lot of people positively, even in a small way, then yes, that is good.[12]

Not every product needs to change the world. Many people do lots of useful things. Just ask yourself, is what I'm doing as useful as it could be? The goal of an organization should be usefulness to society. Not every product will change the world, but if it's making people's lives better, that's great.[13]

This is the same advice I give to my own children: "Follow your heart in terms of what you find interesting or fulfilling to do."[14] I hope they will work extremely hard and become productive contributors to society. I'm also hopeful they will do things

LIVING A PURPOSEFUL LIFE · 33

like engineering, writing books, or just in some way, adding more than they take from the world.[15]

A useful life is worth having lived.[16]

FIGHT FOR THE FUTURE

> Fight for the things that make you excited about the future.
>
> The future will not get here fast enough unless we force it.[17]

I want to make sure there is a good future for humanity. We're on a path to understanding the nature of the universe, the meaning of life. Why are we here; how did we get here?

I came to the conclusion that if we can advance the knowledge of the world—if we can do things that expand the scope and scale of consciousness—then we're better able to ask the right questions and become more enlightened. That's the only way forward.

I use scale *and* scope because we benefit from more consciousness *and* more variety in consciousness. If everyone is thinking about exactly the same things the same way, that may not create new knowledge.[18] I'm motivated by curiosity more than anything.[19]

> I almost had an existential crisis trying to figure out "What does it all mean? What's the purpose of things?"

In college, I would wonder about the future and what areas were really going to have an important impact on the future of humanity as a whole. This wasn't for a paper, just what I thought about in the shower. I came up with five areas.[20]

The three areas I thought would have the biggest *positive* impact on the future of humanity were the internet, the transition to sustainable energy, and space exploration—in particular the extension of life to multiple planets.[21]

The other two, artificial intelligence and rewriting genetics, were a little more uncertain in terms of net benefit. They could be a double-edged sword, and we're not sure which edge is the worst.[22]

I didn't ever expect to be involved in space exploration and expansion, but it seemed important to me even then. Eventually, with the capital from selling PayPal, I was able to work on all three.[23]

Q: What would you say is your most core skill?

I don't worship anything, but I devote myself to the advancement of humanity using technology.

My core personal competence is technology. If something has to be designed or invented and you must ensure the value of the thing you create is greater than the cost of the inputs—that's my core skill.[24]

I look at the future from the standpoint of probabilities. It's a branching stream of probabilities, and actions we can take now affect those probabilities: Accelerate something, slow down another thing, or maybe introduce something new.[25]

You have to ask, What are we doing to move toward the paths likely to make for a good future? That is what I care about. We're all projecting out to the future in some way, and if you think we're going to end up in some terrible situation, that's depressing.[26]

I'm interested in affecting the future in positive ways. I want to build wondrous new technologies where you feel awe when you see it: "How does that even happen? How is that possible?"[27]

I'm not trying to be some sort of savior; that's not my goal. The importance of these things just seems obvious to me. If it seems like the obvious thing to do, I'm not sure why you would do anything else. We want to maximize the happiness of our population, propagate into the future as far as possible, and understand the nature of reality. Everything else follows from that.[28]

Remember the future.[29]

OBSESS FOR SUCCESS

> Doing something I enjoy, which is useful for other people—that gives me satisfaction.[30]

I didn't aspire to create companies as a kid. I just liked computers. Don't start a company because you want to be an entrepreneur or because you want to make money. It is better to approach from this angle: What is a useful thing you could build that you wish existed in the world?[31]

I do not start companies from the standpoint of asking, "What's the best risk-adjusted rate of return?" or what I think could be successful. I just find things that need to happen, and try to make them happen. I thought these things needed to get done. If the money was lost, okay. It was still worth trying.[32]

Try to find an overlap of your talents and what you're interested in. You may have skill in something but don't like doing it. Try to find work that is a good combination of things you are inherently good at but also like doing.[33]

Then, try to get other people to work with you to create that thing. Keep making it better and better. If you create something useful, money will be the result. That's the way a properly working economy rewards the creation of useful goods and services.[34]

Successful entrepreneurs come in all sizes, shapes, and flavors. I'm not sure there's any one particular trait that makes them. However, if there is one to focus on, it would be to have an obsessive nature about the quality of the product. In this context, being obsessive-compulsive is a good thing.[35]

Given that, really really, really liking what you do is a big advantage. It's important to like whatever you're doing. Life is too short to spend it doing something you don't like.[36]

If you like what you're doing, you think about it even when you're not working. It's something your mind is drawn to. If you don't like it, it's much harder to make yourself work.[37]

If you're creating something you love and think other people will love, it's much easier to sacrifice the time and effort. If it doesn't work out, you won't regret it.[38]

> My way of dealing with mental problems is to make sure you really care about what you're doing—and take the pain.[39]

START BEFORE THE WORLD IS READY

> We say the things we believe, even when sometimes those things we believe are delusional.[40]

When you're building a radically new product, people don't know they want it yet, because it's just not in their scope. Around 1946–1948, when they first started making TVs, they did a famous nationwide survey: "Will you ever buy a TV?" and around 96 percent of respondents said, "No."[41]

> In the beginning of Tesla, no one told us they wanted an electric car...I heard that zero times.[42]
>
> If you need encouragement, don't start a company.[43]

Getting people to believe in you and what you're doing is important. In the beginning, very few people will believe in you or what you're doing. Over time, as you make progress, evidence will build. More and more people will start to believe.

CREATE MORE THAN YOU CONSUME

Examine your beliefs of the economy.

The economy is a positive-sum game, a "grow the pie" situation. Those who assume the economy is zero-sum believe the only way to get ahead is by taking things from another.

But obviously the economy today is much, much greater than it was in the past. The economic output per person is massively greater than the past. Obviously the pie has grown, and grown much faster than the population has grown.[44]

> I put a lot of stock in having a grow-the-pie mindset, not a zero-sum mindset.[45]

When I see people (even some smart people) with a bad attitude or doing things that seem morally questionable, it's often because they have a zero-sum mindset.

They don't realize they have a zero-sum mindset, or at least don't realize it consciously. Those who have a zero-sum mindset believe the only way to get ahead is by taking things from others. Those who believe the pie is fixed believe the only way to have more pie is to take someone else's pie. This is obviously false.[46]

In reality, there's a lot of pie. The economic pie is not fixed. It has grown dramatically over time. Make sure you're not operating from a zero-sum mindset, especially without realizing it. It will result in you trying to take things from others, which is not good. It won't benefit you.

> It's much better to work on adding to the economic pie. Create more than you consume.[47]

CREATE MORE THAN YOU CONSUME.

WORK LIKE HELL

> I am wired for war.[48]

Q: Why doesn't the world have more Elon Musks?

If you think you want to be me or do the things I've done...I would say you're probably mistaken. Long periods of my life have been very painful and difficult. I'm not sure people would want to go through that.[49]

The amount I torture myself is next level.[50] You need to have some kind of rage demon in your skull that drives you.[51]

Q: Are you always working?

How many days a year do I not put in some meaningful amount of work? Maybe two or three.[52]

You must be extremely tenacious. Work like hell. You have to put in eighty- to one-hundred-hour weeks every week. This will improve your odds of success.[53]

You need to work. Work hard. Like every waking hour. Particularly if you're starting a company, you need to work super hard. Do the simple math: Somebody else is working fifty hours a week and you're working one hundred. You'll get twice as much done in a year.[54] If other people are putting in forty-hour workweeks and you're putting in one hundred, what takes them a year, you will achieve in four months.[55]

You're not going to create revolutionary cars or rockets in forty hours a week. It just won't work. Colonizing Mars isn't going to happen on forty hours a week.[56]

> Nobody ever changed the world on forty hours a week.[57]

I've done these things because I felt a strong compulsion to do them.[58] I've been burning the candle at both ends with a flamethrower for a very long time.

From 2007 until 2022 was nonstop pain. There was a gun to my head to make Tesla work. Pull a rabbit out of your hat, then pull another rabbit. A stream of rabbits flying through the air. If the next rabbit does not come out, you're dead. It took a toll.

You can't be in a constant fight for survival, always in adrenaline mode, and not have it hurt you. Fighting to survive keeps you going for quite a while.[59]

With that said, I would say this to twenty-something me: I think there's some merit to not being too intense, and enjoying the moment a bit. Occasionally stopping to smell the roses would probably be a good idea.[60]

When we were developing the Falcon One rocket on the Kwajalein Atoll, this beautiful little island in the middle of the Pacific, not once during that entire time did I pause and have a drink on the beach. Now, I realize I should have had a drink with the team on the beach...that would have been fine.[61]

If heat death will inevitably end the universe, it actually **is** all about the journey.[62]

FEEL THE FEAR; DO IT ANYWAY

> Look fear straight in the eye and it will disappear.
>
> The nature of fear is that people don't look at it.
>
> Look at it directly and it will be gone.[63]

Q: How do you think about making a decision when everyone tells you it is a crazy idea?

First of all, I feel fear. It's not as though I have the absence of fear. I feel it quite strongly. But when something is important enough and you believe in it enough, you do it in spite of fear.

You shouldn't think, "I feel fear about this and therefore I shouldn't do it." It's normal to feel fear. If you don't feel fear, you definitely have something mentally wrong. Just feel it and let the importance of your mission drive you to do it anyway.

I also think fatalism is helpful to some degree. If you accept the true probabilities, it diminishes fear. When starting SpaceX, I thought the odds of success were less than 10 percent and I accepted I would probably lose everything. But maybe we would make some progress. If we could just move the ball forward—even if we died—maybe some other company could pick it up and keep moving and our work would still have done good.[64]

> We should not be afraid of doing something just because some amount of tragedy is likely to occur.
>
> If our forefathers had taken that approach, the United States wouldn't exist.[65]

Q: How do you persevere through these hard challenges? Where do you find the strength?

That's not how I think. I think: "This is simply something important. It must get done. We will keep doing it or die trying." I don't need a source of strength for that. Quitting is not in my nature. I don't care about optimism or pessimism. Fuck that. We're going to get it done.[66]

> I definitely emboldened over time.[67]

SEEK THE NATURE OF THE UNIVERSE

> I don't know the meaning of life. I don't think we can answer that question well...**yet**.[68]

We must expand humanity and consciousness to the point where we *are* able to answer that question.[69]

It may be uncomfortable for a lot of people, but I think this is a rational and logical philosophy. Basically saying, "We don't know what the answer is, but let's try to find out."[70]

I think we as humans collectively know part of the answer, but only a tiny part at this point. If we can make civilization last for a million years, we will probably know much more of the answer.[71]

If we date civilization from the first written language, it was about five thousand years ago. This is practically no time at all. If civilization were to last a million more years, we're barely even at the beginning. Future humans will think of us as ancient ancients, like cavemen.[72]

> This is the foundation of my philosophy: I am curious about the nature of the universe.

We can see the archaeological evidence in the fossil record, based on what we know of physics, how we came to be at this point on Earth step by step. But that doesn't explain how the universe came to exist in the first place.[73]

How do a bunch of molecules develop consciousness and feelings? From a physics standpoint, the chain of events from the beginning of the universe to now is quite well understood. There was a bunch of hydrogen gas that turned into complex molecules and now an assemblage of complex molecules—us humans who can feel, talk, and think. Apparently if you leave enough hydrogen gas sitting around long enough, it starts talking to itself. That's basically what happened here.[74]

Assuming you believe the physics, which appear to be true, the universe started off as quarks and electrons and quickly became hydrogen, helium, lithium, most of the periodic table. Mostly hydrogen, though. Then, over a long period of time—13.8 billion years—that hydrogen became sentient.[75]

Where along the path from a bunch of hydrogen to human beings did consciousness start? It's crazy.[76] I wonder, is everything conscious or is nothing conscious? Maybe it's just degrees of consciousness or concentrations of consciousness.[77]

Total collective consciousness is how many people there are times the average amount of consciousness per person. If we can expand consciousness by creating more humans and more digital intelligence, then our opportunity to understand the meaning of life is that much greater. I would call this the philosophy of curiosity—to better understand the nature of reality.[78]

What I think Douglas Adams was saying in his book *The Hitchhiker's Guide to the Galaxy* is "The universe is the answer." We need to figure out what questions to ask about the answer that is the universe. The question is the hard part, and if we can properly frame the question then the answer, relatively speaking, is easy.

We need to expand the scope and scale of consciousness in order to understand what questions to ask of the universe. This is the path forward. If we do, we will be better able to understand the nature of the universe and understand the meaning of life. As just one example, we have to get back to the moon and build a science base there. I think we could learn a lot about the nature of the universe.[79]

THINK LIKE A PHYSICIST

I try to be hyperrational.

If the reasoning fits, and you're not violating the laws of physics, that's the thing you should try to do.

These things just don't seem that crazy to me.[80]

OBSESS OVER TRUTH

> Start somewhere. Then be prepared to question your assumptions, fix what you did wrong, and adapt to reality.[81]

I am obsessed with truth. Obsessed.[82] If you're going to come up with a good solution, the truth is really, really important.[83]

This obsession with truth is why I studied physics, because physics attempts to understand the truth of the universe. Physics is about finding the provable truths of the universe, and finding truths that have predictive power.[84]

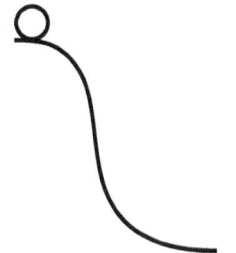

PHYSICS
IS LAW.

EVERYTHING ELSE IS
A RECOMMENDATION.

> Physics is law. Everything else is a recommendation. I've met many people who can break the laws of man, but I have never met anyone who could break the laws of physics.

For me, physics was a natural thing to study. It was intrinsically interesting to understand the nature of the universe. I also studied computer science and information theory to understand logic. (Information theory studies the transmission, processing, extraction, and use of information.) There's an argument that information theory is actually operating at a more fundamental level than physics.[85]

> Truth matters to me a lot. Pathologically, it matters to me.[86]

No matter how smart you are, you will make some number of mistakes. Everyone makes mistakes. It's just a question of how many and how often.[87]

In business and personal life, wishful thinking causes a lot of mistakes. You have to ask whether something is true or not. If something ever feels too easy or doesn't quite make sense...it is probably wishful thinking.[88]

Wishful thinking is a natural human tendency. It's a challenge to tell the difference between believing in a new idea and persevering or pursuing an unrealistic dream. You need to be rigorous in your self-analysis. Focus on something you're confident will have high value to someone else. Be rigorous in making that assessment too.[89]

The real test of any startup is how well it responds to adversity and adapts. When most things start out they don't make much sense, but as long as you adapt quickly you can make the company work.

> Being tenacious and super focused on the truth is extremely important. Look for feedback from all sources.[90]
>
> If you have beliefs that are incompatible with a rocket getting to orbit, the rocket will not get to orbit. Physics is a harsh judge.[91]

Do you have the right fundamental axioms, or truths? Are they relevant? Are you making the right conclusions based on those truths? That's the essence of critical thinking, and yet it is amazing how often people fail to do that. Wishful thinking is innate in the human brain. You want things to be the way you wish them to be, so you tend to filter out information you shouldn't.[92]

That's why I always assume we're losing, even when it looks like we might win.[93]

FIRST-PRINCIPLES THINKING

Q: Where does first-principles thinking come from?

When you want to do something new, you have to apply the physics approach. Physicists discover counterintuitive new things, like quantum mechanics. They do that by thinking from "first principles": building their reasoning from the ground up.[94]

> I would encourage people to use the mental tools of physics and apply them broadly in life. They are the best tools.[95]

The normal way we conduct our lives is reasoning by analogy. That means we do something because it's similar to something else, or what other people are doing.

When you think this way, you only get slight iterations. It's easier to reason by analogy rather than from first principles, so that's what we do most of the time.[96] And in most of life, we should reason by analogy. Otherwise, mentally, you wouldn't be able to get through the day. It would be too much thinking.[97]

But for important things, that kind of thinking is too bound by convention or prior experiences. You will hear, "It's always been done this way," or "Nobody's ever done it." That is a ridiculous way to think.

Don't just follow the trends. You can avoid following trends by thinking with the physics approach, first principles. It's a powerful, powerful method for life in general.

Look at the fundamentals and construct your reasoning from there. Then see if you have a conclusion that works or doesn't work.[98] It might or might not be different from what people have done in the past.[99]

Q: How do you apply first-principles thinking?

Break something down to the most fundamental principles. Start by asking: What am I most confident is true at a foundational level? That sets your axiomatic base. Then you reason up from there. Then you check your conclusions against the axiomatic truths.

For instance, to approach any new technology problem, make sure you're not violating physics with a first-principles analysis. A basic question in physics would be: Am I violating conservation of energy or momentum? If so, it's not going to work. That's just to establish if this idea is possible.[100]

It's hard to think this way. It takes a lot of effort. But if you're trying to do something new, it's the best way to think.[101]

Q: How have you applied first-principles thinking to building companies?

Here's an example from early in building Tesla. People said battery packs were too expensive to make cheap electric cars. They assumed they would always be expensive, because they had been in the past. That's pretty dumb. If you applied that reasoning to everything new, then you would never try anything new. "Oh, nobody wants a car. Horses are great; we're used to them. They can eat grass. There's lots of grass all over the place. There's no gasoline available. So people will never buy gas cars." People did say that, a lot.

People assumed batteries for electric vehicles would always cost $600 per kilowatt hour. The first-principles approach to battery costs is this: What are the batteries made of? What are the materials that make up the batteries? What is the market value of those material constituents?

It's got cobalt, nickel, aluminum, carbon, some polymers for separation, and a steel can. Okay, what if we bought that amount of material at the London Metal Exchange? What would each of those things cost? Oh, geez, it's only $80 per kilowatt hour. So clearly, we just need to think of clever ways to take those materials and combine them into the shape of a battery cell. That's how I knew it was possible to build batteries much much cheaper than anyone else realized.[102]

> Great differences in technology exist in the world, which even hardcore technologists are unaware of.
>
> What is simple in one arena is often profound in another.[103]

The first-principles approach is a good way to understand what new things are possible. It doesn't mean you'll be successful, but at least you can determine if success is one of the possibilities, and that is important. This is how I decided to start SpaceX.[104]

First-principles thinking built SpaceX. Most people think, "Historically, all rockets have been expensive. Therefore, in the future, all rockets will be expensive." But that's not true.[105] This is where it's helpful to use the analytical approach again.[106]

The way we applied first-principles thinking to rocketry was asking, "What are the materials that go into a rocket?"[107] A rocket is made from aluminum, titanium, copper, and carbon fiber. Break it down further and ask, "How much of each material is used? Now, what is the cost of all these raw components?"[108]

If you have them stacked on the floor and could wave a magic wand to create the rocket, what would the cost of the rocket be? We imagine the cost of rearranging the atoms was zero.[109]

That's going to set the floor of the cost of the rocket. I call this the "magic wand number," the hypothetical best-case scenario. For rockets, that turned out to be a relatively small number, well under 5 percent of the current cost, in some cases closer to 1 or 2 percent.[110] The manufacturing must be very inefficient if the raw material cost is only 1 or 2 percent of the finished product.[111]

I was able to see a great deal of room for improvement.[112] Now our challenge was to figure out how to get the atoms in the right shape more efficiently.[113]

That first-principles thought process around the rocket became general purpose for all parts. I call it "The Idiot Index."

How much more does a finished product cost than the cost of its materials? If a part or product had a high Idiot Index, we could cut the cost with more efficient manufacturing techniques.[114]

A component that costs $1,000 when the aluminum it was made of costs only ten dollars likely has a design that is too complex or an inefficient manufacturing process. If the ratio is high, you're an idiot.

One part of the rocket, the half nozzle jacket, cost $13,000. But it was only made of $200 worth of steel. I expect all my engineers to know all the best and worst parts in their systems as judged by the idiot index at all times.[115]

That's what I mean by thinking about things from a first-principles standpoint. If I had analyzed it by analogy and said, "What are all other rocket companies doing? What do their rockets cost? What historically have other rockets cost?" That is reasoning by analogy, but *it really doesn't illustrate what the true potential is*.[116]

The first-principles approach is a good way to figure out counterintuitive solutions. It was a helpful thing to learn.[117]

THINKING IN LIMITS

Another good physics tool is thinking about things "in the limit." Take a particular idea and imagine scaling it to a very large or very small number. How do things change?[118]

The Boring Company is a great example. A common criticism of the idea of tunnels is: The tunnel will get used up and there will still be traffic congestion. They don't realize there's no real limit to *how many* levels of tunnel you can have. You can go much farther deep underground than you can build up. The deepest mines are much deeper than the tallest buildings are tall.

Ever notice that cities are built in 3D, but roads are only built in 2D? You could build roads in 3D by building tunnels under cities.[119] You can alleviate any amount of urban congestion with a 3D tunnel network.[120]

But, it's difficult and expensive to dig tunnels the way they're currently done. The LA subway extension cost roughly a billion dollars per mile to build.[121]

> If you do just two things, you can get approximately an order of magnitude improvement in tunneling.
>
> But I think you can even go beyond that.[122]

We need at least a tenfold improvement in the cost per mile of tunneling. The first thing to do is to cut the tunnel diameter. According to current regulations, a single road-lane tunnel has to be twenty-six to twenty-eight feet in diameter. But if you shrink that diameter to twelve feet, the area goes down by a factor of four. This is a huge improvement, because the cost of tunneling scales with the area. That's almost a half-order of magnitude (4–5x) improvement in cost per mile right there.[123]

Currently, tunneling machines work for half the time, then stop. The other half of the time is putting in reinforcements for the tunnel wall. If you design the machine instead to do continuous tunneling *and* reinforcing, that will give you a factor of two improvement. Combine those and that's a factor of eight.[124]

These machines are also far from being at their power or thermal limits, so we should jack up the power to the machine. We can get at least another factor of two there, maybe even four or five. Currently, we're not even close to the limits of tunneling technology.[125]

Q: How does thinking in limits apply to manufacturing?

Let's say we're trying to figure out why a part or product is expensive. Is it because of something foolish, or just because production volume is too low?[126]

Ask, "If our volume was a million units per year, would it still be expensive?" If it's still expensive at a million units a year, then volume is not the reason why your part is expensive. Maybe something's wrong with the design. Maybe you can change the part to something not fundamentally expensive. That's thinking about things to the limit.[127]

If you are really good at manufacturing *and* producing at a high volume, you can make anything for a cost that asymptotically approaches the raw material value of the components, plus any intellectual property you need to license. It's a hard thing to do, but it is possible.[128]

Q: How does thinking in the limit apply to design?

When designing a product, people often start designing with the tools, parts, and methods they are familiar with. That's their default. That will lead to a product that can be made with those tools and methods, but it is unlikely to be the perfect product.[129]

The other way to think is to imagine the platonic ideal of the perfect product or technology. What is the perfect arrangement of atoms that would be the best possible product? Now try to figure out how to get the atoms in that shape.[130]

Think through things in both directions. What can we build with the tools that we have? But also, what does the "theoretically perfect" product look like?[131]

The idea of the "theoretically perfect" product is going to be a moving target because as you learn more, the definition for that perfect product will change. You don't actually know what the perfect product is, but you can approximate a *more* perfect product. Then ask, "What tools, methods, or materials do we need to create to get the atoms in that shape?" People rarely think this way. But thinking in limits is a powerful tool.[132]

> Impossible is a strong word. It's just a strong word. I approach things from a physics standpoint, and the word impossible is more or less banned in physics.[133]

At SpaceX especially, we often consider what's possible within the absurd. If my team says something is impossible, I try to open their minds to new potential solutions by asking, "What would it take?"[134]

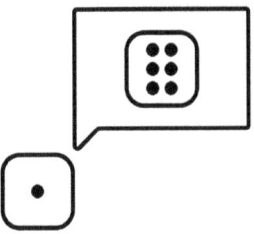

IT IS OK TO BE WRONG, JUST DON'T
BE CONFIDENT AND WRONG.

ASPIRE TO BE LESS WRONG

The mental tools of physics are powerful. They tell us to assume we're wrong and that our goal is to be less wrong. Aspire to be less wrong. I don't think you're going to succeed every day in being less wrong. But if you can succeed in being less wrong most of the time, you're doing great.[135]

> It's OK to be wrong. Just don't be confident and wrong.[136]

Aspirationally, you want to believe things proportionate to the evidence. Not inversely proportional to the evidence.[137]

> Most people can learn a lot more than they think they can.
>
> They sell themselves short by not trying.[138]

Read books, because the data rate of reading is much greater than when somebody is speaking. What's the output rate of speech? A couple hundred bits per second, maybe a few thousand per second if you're going full tilt. You can get several times that by reading. The main reason I didn't go to lectures in college was because the data rate was too slow.[139]

> I encourage you to read a lot of books. Just read.
> Try to ingest as much information as you can.

I was always really interested in reading. When I was a kid, I read everything I could get my hands on.[140] Around nine or ten I ran out of things to read in our house, so in desperation I read the encyclopedia—which turned out to be a good idea. I found all sorts of things I didn't even know existed—a lot, obviously.

I'd recommend everyone read or skim through the condensed version of the *Encyclopedia Britannica*. You can always skip subjects. If you read a few paragraphs and know you're not interested, just jump to the next one.[141]

Develop good general knowledge, so you at least have a rough "lay of the land" of the full knowledge landscape. Read a broad range of material. How can you know what you're really interested in if you're not at least doing a broad, light exploration of the knowledge landscape?[142]

As a kid, I played historical strategy video games, like *Civilization*. This shows you how civilization formed. Through the technology tree, you invent different things. You'd invent literacy, democracy, and gunpowder. You start to realize, "Oh wow, there are stages to technology. You can't have democracy without creating literacy." There are stages of technology and development of ideas. That's a helpful framework.[143]

It is important to view knowledge as a semantic tree. Make sure you understand the fundamental principles (the trunk and big branches) before you get into the leaves (the details), then there is something for them to hang on to.[144]

Some ideas come from reading about a sad trend in technology. When I read about the Concorde being retired, I was like, "Jeez, we don't even have supersonic transport anymore. That's terrible." I never had a chance to fly on the Concorde. That seemed like a terrible thing, so I started reading about it.

I learned the Concorde was designed back in the sixties. Aerodynamics have improved a great deal since then, with computational fluid dynamics. Engine efficiencies have improved massively. Even if you just change the engines on the Concorde, you could double the range or thereabouts. I thought, *Well, what if we could figure out an efficient design that could make it economically competitive to have a supersonic aircraft?* I started looking into it more and did the math on all of it.[145]

You can get super efficient and super fast when electric aircraft have vertical takeoff and landing, and go supersonic. We could make a breakthrough aircraft several generations beyond what currently exists.[146]

Diving into SpaceX and Tesla, I had to learn how to make hardware. I'd never seen a CNC machine or laid out carbon fiber. I didn't know any of those things, but if you read books and talk to experts, you can pick them up quickly.[147] I started going to the Palo Alto public library to read about rocket engineering and started calling experts, asking to borrow their old engine manuals.[148]

Most people self-limit their ability to learn. It's pretty straightforward—just read books and talk to people.[149]

The physics background is helpful as the foundation. But in rocketry I am self-taught, meaning I don't have an aerospace degree. I just read a lot of books and talked to a lot of people.[150]

> Talk to people from different walks of life, in different industries, professions, and skills. Try to learn as much as possible. Search for meaning.[151]

THE VALUE OF ENGINEERING

I spend 80 percent of my time on engineering.[152]

ENGINEERING IS MAGIC

Engineering is, for all intents and purposes, magic, and who wouldn't want to be a magician?[153]

Q: What drew you to engineering?

I have a physics background and grew up in an engineering-centric household. I'm still more an engineer than anything else.[154]

My dad is an extremely talented electrical and mechanical engineer. We built model airplanes and circuit boards together when I was a kid. He tutored me, and I didn't even know it at the time.[155] I also did things like make model rockets. In South Africa, there were no premade rockets. I had to go to the chemist to get the ingredients for rocket fuel, mix it, and put it in a pipe.[156]

There were lots of "engineery" things around me. When I asked for an explanation, I got the true explanation of how things work.[157] When I was a little kid, I was really scared of the dark. But I came to understand "dark" just means the absence of photons in the visible wavelength—four hundred to seven hundred nanometers. I thought, well it's silly to be afraid of a lack of photons. Then I wasn't afraid of the dark anymore.[158]

I was very technology oriented as a kid growing up in South Africa.[159] With our first computer came books to teach yourself programming. This was the coolest thing I'd ever seen. When I was about twelve, I started programming and selling my own games to buy new games. I was hooked. I'd spend money on better computers, *Dungeons & Dragons* modules, and things like that. I was nerdmaster3000.[160]

I wasn't that much of a loner, but I was quite bookish. I was reading all the time. I would be reading, working on my computer, reading comics, that kind of thing.[161]

When I was young, I wasn't sure what I was going to do when I got older. I thought the idea of inventing things would be cool, because I read a quote from Arthur C. Clarke: "A sufficiently advanced technology is indistinguishable from magic." That's really true.

If you go back three hundred years, you'd be burned at the stake for things we take for granted today. Being able to fly is crazy. Being able to see over long distances, communicate, and instantly access all the world's information from almost anywhere on the earth. This would all be considered magic in times past. It actually goes beyond that. Many things we take for granted today weren't imagined in times past, even in the realm of magic.

I thought if I could advance technology, that would be like being a magician. That would be really cool.[162]

At one point, I was thinking about doing physics as a career. But to really advance physics these days, you need new data. Physics is fundamentally governed by the progress of engineering.

There is always debate about, "Which is better, engineers or scientists? Aren't scientists better? Wasn't Einstein the smartest person?" Personally, I think engineering is better because without engineering, you do not have any new data. You hit a limit.

You can be smart within the context of the limits of the data you have, but unless you have a way to get more data, you can't make progress. Galileo engineered the telescope, which allowed him to see Jupiter had moons. If you want to advance civilization, you must address the limiting factor. The limiting factor is the engineering. Therefore, you must address the engineering.[163]

I certainly admire the discoveries of the great scientists. They're creating a deeper understanding of how the universe already works. That's cool—but the universe, in a way, already knows that. They're discovering what already exists.[164]

Science is discovering the essential truths about what exists in the universe.

Engineering is about creating things that have never existed before.[165]

ENGINEERING WINS WARS

In Sun Tzu's *The Art of War*, there is no chapter on technology. It is an interesting book I've read many times. It's packed with wisdom, but there should be a chapter saying: "If you have a decisive technological advantage, you can win with minimal casualties to your side."[166]

Technology plays a much stronger role in war than is generally understood: technology viewed in the broadest sense, including a better phalanx, or spears made of bronze, iron, or steel. These can be big differences.[167]

> The Romans won their wars through technology.[168]

One of the advantages Romans had was good metallurgy. Their swords were martensitic (an improvement over austenitic metallurgy), so they were stronger. The Romans were often fighting opponents whose swords would basically bend over a Roman sword. If you're in a sword fight and your sword bends like a noodle…big disadvantage.[169]

The Romans were great engineers. Even things like building roads gave them a military advantage. If you're trying to march an army somewhere fast, roads beat the heck out of a small winding path through the forest.[170]

But when fighting outside the Roman empire, they sometimes lost their wars because of their opponent's technology. When the Romans fought the Scythians, they did not have a good counter to mounted war archers, especially if they got lured into flat terrain. They were pretty much helpless against the technology of a mounted archer.[171]

> **When there's a rapid change in the rate of technology, engineering plays a pivotal role.**

If there is a big difference in the technologies—even if the other side has more people, better generals, and is smarter—the side with the advanced technology will win.[172]

The technology war of fighters and bombers during World War II is fascinating. The US completely crushed it on bombers at the end of the war, but they didn't start out that way. At the start of World War II in the Pacific, entire US squadrons were sometimes shot down with zero Japanese losses. A total KO. The US fighters at the beginning of World War II were not good either. Their tactics were terrible, the aircraft were terrible, and the training was incorrect, too.[173]

It's interesting to see where they started out and how fast things innovated. There was impressive design work by many countries: Japan, the US, Germany, UK, Russia, and others had some impressive fighter designs.[174]

It was a constant technological rock-paper-scissors game. One country would make a plane, another made a new plane to beat that one, then another country would make an even newer plane. What really matters is the *pace* of innovation.[175]

When the rate of change of technology is high enough, or there is a big technological difference between one side and the other, then that technology dominates and you get a lopsided victory.[176]

Many books on the strategy of war actually don't address technology, or do only in a tangential manner. But obviously, if there is an overwhelming technological advantage, that side will win even if the odds are dramatically stacked against them.[177]

To use an extreme example (a limit case), if you can shoot lasers from space to any spot on the ground by just pointing at it, it would not matter if you're fighting Julius Caesar, Heinz Guderian, or Napoleon. They just got lasered from space.[178]

Most battles in history, because technology moved slowly, were more about maneuvering, tactics, and strategy. But when there's technological discontinuity, it fundamentally changes the whole situation. Wars in the modern era are very much technology race wars. How fast can we create new technology? The best example would be the nuclear bomb. Anyone who made nuclear bombs first, won. That's it. End of story.[179]

That was the reason for the US Manhattan Project. People think it was a government project. I'd like to emphasize that it was a creation of the physics community more than it was the government. The government supported it, but it was a decision and creation from the physics community. Without them, it would not have happened.[180]

They simply came to the conclusion that they couldn't let Hitler have the bomb. So they made it first to be certain of it.

There isn't a better example of a super weapon—anyone who gets it wins.[181]

Play to win, or don't play at all.[182]

ENGINEERING CREATES VALUE

My mind feels like a wild storm. I have a fountain of ideas. I have more ideas than I could possibly execute. Innovation is not the problem. Execution is the problem.[183]

There is never a shortage of ideas. I find ideas to be somewhat trivial, but the execution of good ideas is extremely difficult. Prototypes are easy; production is hard. Production and being cash flow positive is excruciating pain. Product ideas are nearly irrelevant.[184]

You only build value in a company if you do hard work to solve tough problems. That's why companies are valuable. It's why they should be valuable, and largely why they are.

Tesla is a hardcore technology company. We do serious engineering. We do real manufacturing as well. We do hardcore manufacturing. Coils of aluminum and plastic pellets go into one end of the factory and cars come out the other. We did all the vehicle engineering, all the powertrain engineering, all the software. The evidence for us solving hard engineering problems is that Toyota, Daimler, and Mercedes buy electric powertrains from us. If it was easy, they would do it.[185]

> The idea of going to Mars is not hard; that's irrelevant.
>
> Getting to Mars is the hard part.

PART II

ULTRA HARDCORE WORK

To those who quietly help advance the causes we mutually believe in, knowing advancing the cause is the only reward: thank you.[186]

WHAT IT TAKES

If conventional thinking makes your mission impossible, then unconventional thinking is necessary.[187]

TAKE RESPONSIBILITY

> I am CEO of these companies because I feel I'm responsible for them, not because it's the best thing for my quality of life.[188]

I want to emphasize that sometimes—in fact, most of the time—I get way too much credit or attention for what I do. I'm just the visible element. The reason these companies are successful is because we have extremely talented people at all levels making it happen.[189]

I didn't expect to be CEO of these big companies. It just sort of happened that way.[190] It was never my intent to run Tesla. Running two companies is quite a burden. Sometimes when people think of being a CEO, they imagine granting themselves lots of vacation and doing fun things. It doesn't work that way. What you actually get as CEO is a distillation of the worst things going on in the company.[191]

Particularly, if you're the CEO, you work on all the worst problems in the company. There's no point in spending time on things that are going right, so you only spend time on things that are going wrong. Specifically, the things other people can't fix. The most pernicious and painful problems.[192]

Q: How do you manage through failure?

Managing through big failures is painful and difficult. It feels terrible. The company looks at me to rally them, so I do. But I feel terrible. Failure is a punch in the gut. Even when you've got a lot of smart people working super hard to minimize the probability of failure, it's still there. And it's quite significant.[193]

Given the options, I prefer to learn from success.[194]

EARN DEEP UNDERSTANDING

I wanted to know how the universe works and how the economy works. So, I studied physics and economics. You need to be able to bring a lot of people together to create something. It's difficult to do something as just an individual, especially for a significant technology.[195]

I was concerned if I didn't study business I would be forced to work for someone who did, because they would know special things I didn't know. I didn't like the sound of that, so I made sure I knew those things, too.[196]

Physics gave me the basics, a good analytical framework.[197] Physics was rigorous, and we learned a lot of math. Later, I was in an advanced securities analysis class in the business school, and they were teaching people matrix math. I realized if you can do physics math, then business math is super easy.[198]

> My goals were to engineer products by having a feel for the physics and to never work for a boss with a business degree.[199]

One reason SpaceX could move so quickly is I made both the engineering decisions and the spending decisions together in one brain. In most companies, those decisions require at least two different people.

There's some engineering guy who's trying to convince a finance guy that this money should be spent. But the finance guy doesn't understand engineering, so he can't tell if this is a good way to spend money or not. Plus, they may not trust each other. I'm making the engineering and spending decisions together with all the information in one place. My brain trusts itself.[200]

I'm head engineer, chief designer, and CEO at SpaceX, so I don't have to cave to some money guy. I encounter CEOs who don't know the details of their technology, and that's ridiculous to me.[201]

> To make the right decisions, you need to understand something at a detailed level.[202]

SLEEP ON THE FACTORY FLOOR

I've done many many stretches of one-hundred-hour weeks—true one-hundred-hour weeks, sleeping roughly six hours per day. I would not recommend that. That's for emergencies, not all the time.

During difficult times at Tesla I've had to do it, and sometimes at the beginning of my earliest startups I did that. I wouldn't leave the office. I would sleep under my desk and work seven days a week. Sometimes it's necessary for success, or to avoid failure.[203]

Tesla is pretty far up there in terms of work ethic, anywhere in the world. The Tesla work ethic is substantially greater than any other large car or manufacturing company in the US, that I'm aware of.[204]

If there was a crisis situation, I slept on the floor. Most of the time I did not sleep in a conference room because people could not see me in the conference room—I slept on the floor in the factory. Otherwise how would people know? They wouldn't. Seeing is believing. I slept on the floor outside the conference room so they could see I was there.[205]

When the team is being asked to work super hard, I have to be right there with them and they have to see it. If I fall asleep in the middle of the factory floor at four in the morning and wake up four hours later, they see that. They are like, "If the CEO is willing to take that level of pain, I can do it too."[206]

It was a world of hurt. I would wake up smelling like oil and iron filings. It was rough. But I was asking people to really go all out. I can't expect them to go all out if I'm not doing the same.[207]

FRONTLINE LEADERSHIP

Think about war. Do you want the general in some ivory tower or on the front lines? The troops fight harder if they see the general on the front lines. Nobody bleeds for the prince in the palace. Get out there on the front line. Show them that you care and that you're not in some plush office somewhere.[208]

If they see the general out on the battlefield, the troops are going to be motivated. Wherever Napoleon was, that's where his armies would be at their best. Even if I don't do anything but show up, they'll look at me and know I wasn't spending all night partying.[209]

> Never ask your troops to do something you're not willing to do.
>
> Whatever the people at the front lines are doing, I try to do it at least a few times myself.[210]

It is my firm belief that the separation of the workplace into "executives" and "employees" does not create a good working environment. We want to create a system of equality without artificial barriers, so someone can start as a trainee and one day lead the entire company.

This is why we eliminate all special privileges of executives. Everyone has equal access to parking, eating at the same tables, and there are no management offices. I am convinced that managers should work at the forefront, in the same work environment as the entire team. Even though I run a company, I still do not have my own office and often move my workplace to the most challenging area in the factory.

Managers should always take care of their team before they take care of themselves. The supervisor is there to serve his team, not the other way round.[211]

All technical managers must have hands-on experience. For example, managers of software teams must spend at least 20 percent of their time coding. Solar roof managers must spend time on the roofs doing installations. Otherwise, they are like a cavalry leader who can't ride a horse or a general who can't use a sword.[212]

Always be smashing your ego. Internalize responsibility. Whether you're a CEO or any other role, do whatever it takes to succeed.[213]

A major failure mode is a high ego-to-ability ratio. If your ego-to-ability ratio gets too high, then you've broken the feedback loop to reality.[214]

In AI terms, you'll break your reinforcement learning (RL) loop. You want to have a strong RL loop, which means internalizing responsibility and minimizing ego.[215]

> Do whatever the task is, whether grand or humble.[216]

ADVERSITY FORGES STRENGTH

> There is a great quote from Winston Churchill: "If you're going through hell, keep going."[217]

Q: Do you think overcoming challenges is something innate in your personality?

I was driven as a kid, very willful. One story I remember: At age six, I was grounded for some reason. I don't remember why, but I felt it was unjust. I really wanted to go to my cousin's birthday party.[218] I escaped from my nanny and walked across the city.

I was just learning to read, so I could barely read the road signs. This was foolish, and something terrible could have happened. But I was so determined I walked clear across the capital city of South Africa at six years old.[219]

It was ten or twelve miles, much farther than I realized, and it took me about four hours. As my mom was leaving the party with my brother and sister, she saw me walking down the road and freaked out. So I climbed a tree and refused to come down until she promised not to punish me.[220]

> I seem to have a high, innate drive, and that's been true even since I was a little kid.

When I was five or six, I thought I was insane. It became clear other people's minds weren't exploding with ideas all the time. I felt strange. It's hard to turn it off. It might sound great when it is on. But what if it doesn't turn off? It's like a never-ending explosion.[221]

I was the youngest kid in my grade, so I was quite small. I was kind of a smart aleck, too. It was a recipe for disaster. I'd get called every name in the book and beaten up. Being small and having violent bullies is a bad situation.[222]

There was a level of violence in my childhood that wouldn't be tolerated in any American school. It was like *Lord of the Flies*. There were a couple of gangs that were pretty evil, and I was one of their chosen victims. Partly because I stuck up for another kid they were relentless on, that made me a target.[223]

The place where I grew up in South Africa was very violent. Fighting was normal, it was part of the culture.[224] It'll certainly toughen you up; that's for sure. I was in a lot of fights I didn't want to be in. I got beaten up really badly in a few of them. I was in real hardcore street fights, from about six to sixteen.[225]

> I was almost beaten to death—within an inch of my life at one point.[226]

I got to a reasonably good size around fifteen, and around sixteen they stopped trying to beat me up, because it didn't work out so well for them anymore.[227]

People say they're worried about the damage of words. People worried about words have never been punched in the face. Once you've been punched in the face, real hard, right on the nose—you'll take any words over that.[228]

Adversity shaped me. My pain threshold became very high.[229]

EAT GLASS AND STARE INTO THE ABYSS

> When starting a company, usually the beginning is fun.
>
> Then, it's hellish for a number of years.[230]

You have to be focused on the short term and money coming in when creating a company, because otherwise the company will die. People think, "Oh, creating a company will be fun." It's not. There are periods of fun, and there are periods where it's just awful.

You have to feel quite compelled to start a company. You must have a high pain threshold. My friend Bill Lee says, "Starting a company is like eating glass and staring into the abyss." There's some truth to that.[231]

"Staring into the abyss'" means you're going to be constantly facing the extermination of the company. Most startups fail. It's like 90 percent—it could be 99 percent of startups fail. You're constantly saying, "If I don't get this right, the company will die." This can be quite stressful.[232]

"Eating glass" means you've got to work on the problems the company needs you to work on, not the problems you want to work on. You end up working on problems you wish you *weren't* working on. That's "eating glass," and it goes on for a long time.[233]

We were facing imminent death at SpaceX, Tesla, and SolarCity for a long time. We're no longer staring directly into the abyss, which is great. It is there in the distance, but I'm not staring right at it. There's always going to be some amount of glass that has to be chewed. But it's less and less as time goes by.[234]

> If you don't eat the glass, you're not going to be successful.[235]

Q: How do you keep your focus on the big picture when you're constantly faced with being bankrupt in a month?

A very small percentage of mental energy is spent on the big picture. You know where you're generally heading, and the actual path is going to be a zigzag in that direction. You're trying not to deviate too far from the path you want to be on, but you have to, to some degree.[236]

Failure is not good. Failure is bad. But if something is important enough, then you do it, even though the risk of failure is high. My advice for somebody who wants to start a company: Bear in mind, the most likely outcome is failure. Reconcile yourself to that strong possibility, and only if you still feel compelled to, do it.[237]

That said, many people fear starting a company *too* much. What's the worst that could happen? You're not gonna starve to death; you're not gonna die of exposure—really, what's the worst that could happen?[238]

BUILDING EXCEPTIONAL TEAMS

> The most important thing is to attract great people. Whether you are creating a company or joining a company, find an amazing group that you really respect.[239]

A GROUP WITH A GOAL

A company is just a bunch of people coming together to create a product or service. There's no such thing as "a business," just a group pursuing a goal.[240]

How talented and hardworking that group is, and the degree to which they are focused cohesively in a good direction, will determine the success of the company. If you're creating a company, or if you're joining a company, the most important thing is to attract great people.[241]

A company is essentially a cybernetic collective of people and machines. This collective is far smarter than an individual.[242] That's what a company is, and there are different levels of complexity in the way companies are formed.[243]

Obviously, one person can't build a whole rocket, engines, launchpad, and everything. That's impossible. We have thousands of people at SpaceX. By piecing it out to different people and using our collection of computers, tools, and machines we can make lots of rockets, launch them into orbit, dock with the International Space Station, and more.[244]

People sometimes forget a company is just a group of people gathered together to make products for fellow human beings.

As long as they make great products, the company will have great value.[245]

To create a company, you have to convince others to join you in your effort. You have to convince them there is a reasonable chance of success and if there is success, the reward will be commensurate with the effort.

> If you're going to create a company, the first thing you should try to do is create a working prototype.[246]

When starting a company, create a demonstration, a mock-up, or a sketch. This helps people envision it. Try to get to that point as soon as possible, then iterate to make it as real as possible as fast as possible.[247]

It doesn't sink in for people until you actually have a physical object they can use. Even when you can show something works on paper, and the calculations are clear, it's not the same.[248]

Anything can look good on PowerPoint. If you have an actual demonstration, even in primitive form, it is much more effective in convincing people.[249]

> Fundamentally, if you don't have a compelling product at a compelling price, you don't have a great company.[250]

CREATE A CULTURE OF BUILDERS

> I consider one of my core responsibilities as CEO is to have an environment where great engineers can flourish.[251]

I don't think I manage smart people; they manage themselves. If someone is smart and talented, they can go anywhere and do anything, anytime.[252]

I say, "Look, this is the goal we're after. Do you agree with this goal? If you do, then let's try to get it done."

I'll provide my opinion along the way. But it's rare for me to actually insist on a particular thing. Once in a while I'll say, "You have to trust me on this one. We have to do this, and if it turns out to be a bad decision, we can all hold it against me in the future."[253]

Another important principle: You want everyone to be able to think like the chief engineer. They need to understand the system at a high level, well enough to know when they are making a bad optimization.[254]

Since a company is a group of people assembled to create a product or service, the ability to attract and motivate great people is critical to the success of a company. That's the purpose of a company. People sometimes forget this elementary truth.

If you're able to get talented, hard-working people to join the company, work together, and have a relentless sense of perfection toward a common goal, you will end up with a great product. If you have a great product, lots of people will buy it, and the company will be successful.[255]

That's why our most important consideration is recruiting the best people. The output of any company is the vector sum of the people within it. If we attract the most talented people over time and our direction is correctly aligned, we will prevail.[256]

> A small group of technically strong people will always beat a large group of moderately strong people.[257]

What you see at SpaceX is the result of an incredible team. Supertalented people who work like crazy to advance technology. They make this happen. My role is to make sure they have an environment where their talents can come to the fore. I can't tell you how honored and grateful I am to work with such a great team.[258]

> Do everything you can to gather great people.[259]

Many companies suppress their talented, driven engineers. Some are suppressed by being so comfortable they don't produce much. There are a few places in Silicon Valley with good engineers—but what are they producing? The output of that engineering talent seems low, though maybe they are enjoying themselves.

Tesla is not like that. We're demanding. You're going to get a lot done and it's going to be cool work, but it's not going to be easy. At Tesla, a superb engineer's talents are used to a greater degree than anywhere else.[260]

Tesla has been like a whole series of startups. So far almost all have been quite successful, so we must be doing something right.[261]

Only exceptional performance constitutes a passing grade.[262]

RECRUIT FOR EXCEPTIONAL ABILITY

> When hiring, I look for evidence of exceptional ability, or at least exceptional aspiration.

Sometimes these things get messed up in recruiting. I sometimes wonder, "If Nikola Tesla applied to Tesla, would we even give him an interview?" It's not clear. They might say, "This guy came from some weird college in Eastern Europe, he's got some odd mannerisms, we don't know if we should give him an interview." I worry that's what we'd do. Our response should be, "Man, Nikola Tesla, this kid's super smart. What does he want? We'll pay him anything!"[263]

I always ask my teams to give a lot of thought to who should join. I recommend paying close attention to people who haven't completed their grad or even undergrad, but are obviously brilliant. Better to have them join before they achieve a breakthrough.[264]

You've got to be willing to recruit hard for excellent people. When I was interviewing Bülent Altan for SpaceX, I told him, "I heard you don't want to move to Los Angeles because your wife works for Google in San Francisco. Well, I just talked to Larry Page, and they're going to transfer your wife down to LA. So what are you going to do now?" He said he would come work for SpaceX.[265]

I have a great ability to tell if someone is a good engineer or not. And I am good at optimizing the efficiency of an engineering team. It helps that I'm quite good at engineering in general.[266]

In interviews, I ask people to tell me the story of their career and some of the tougher problems they dealt with, how they dealt with those, and how they made decisions at key transition points. Usually that's enough for me to get a good gut feeling about someone. What I'm really looking for is evidence of exceptional ability. Did they face difficult problems and overcome them?

Usually the person who had to struggle with the problem really understands it and they don't forget if it was difficult. Ask them detailed questions about it, and they'll know the answers. A person who was not responsible for that accomplishment will not know the details.[267]

RETAIN ONLY SPECIAL FORCES

I worked very hard to collect the right expertise when starting SpaceX. I tried hard to find a great chief engineer for the rocket, but good chief engineers wouldn't join and there is no point in hiring the bad ones. I ended up being chief engineer of the rocket. If I could have found somebody better, maybe we would have had fewer than three failures.[268]

> Wherever the smartest, most driven people are choosing to work, that company is going to win.[269]

My philosophy for companies in the startup phase is a "Special Forces" approach. The minimum passing grade is excellent. I believe that's the culture companies need to have if they're going to become successful.[270]

Q: Is building great teams and products just a question of being well funded?

It's not like if we just had more money we could spend it effectively on R&D. That's not how it works. If there was a factory producing excellent engineers, that would be true. Except this factory doesn't exist. It's incredibly difficult to find the right talent, integrate them into an organization, and have it work effectively. Money is not the constraint.

There are only a small number of excellent people, and they're hard to find. Engineers especially.[271] At the end of the day, the competitiveness of any company is a function of the most talented and driven people. That is the team that's going to win.[272]

> **The fundamental limitation is exceptional engineers. There are not that many.**[273]

Having a strong sense of purpose will attract the very best talent in the world. If the work is enjoyable, the financial rewards are good, *and* the product will change the world—that's a pretty powerful set of motivators.[274]

I've made several hiring decisions where I valued intellect over heart and I think that was a mistake. I have tried to adjust accordingly. It matters whether somebody is a good person.[275]

One test for assessing someone's character is to look at the character of their friends and associates. While people can put up a mask themselves for their character, their friends and associates will not. You can judge a person's character by their associates and to some degree by their enemies. If evil people hate you, you might be doing something right.[276]

> **When hiring, look for people with the right attitude. Skills can be taught. Attitude changes require a brain transplant.**

FEEDBACK OVER FEELINGS

> Physics does not care about hurt feelings. It cares about whether you got the rocket right.[277]

All bad news should be given loudly and often. Good news can be said quietly and once.[278]

I give people hardcore feedback, but I try to always focus on the substance of the discussion. I try to criticize the action, not the person. We all make mistakes. What matters is whether a person has a good feedback loop, can seek criticism from others, and can improve.[279]

It's not your job to make people on your team love you. In fact, that's counterproductive. I had a manager who would not fire anyone. I told him, "You can't tell people they have to get their shit together, and when they don't get their shit together—nothing happens to them."

Camaraderie is dangerous. It makes it hard for people to challenge each other's work. There is a tendency to not want to throw a colleague under the bus. That needs to be avoided.

Wanting to be everyone's friend leads you to care too much about the emotions of the individual in front of you rather than caring about the success of the whole enterprise. Focusing on that one individual can lead to a far greater number of people being hurt.[280]

I think it's a real weakness to want to be liked. A real weakness.

And I do not have that.[281]

DESIGNING THE ORGANIZATION

It must be okay for people to talk directly and make the right thing happen.[282]

REMOVE ORGANIZATIONAL BOUNDARIES

> In any product, you can see the errors in the organization's structure. They will manifest themselves in the product.

A major source of issues is poor communication between departments. The way to solve this is to allow free flow of information between all levels.

There are two schools of thought about how information should flow within companies. The most common way is chain of command. That means you always flow communication through your manager. The problem with this approach is that, while it serves to enhance the power of the manager, it fails to serve the company.

If, in order to get something done between departments, an individual contributor has to talk to their manager, who talks to a director, who talks to a VP, who talks to another VP, who talks to a director, who talks to a manager, who talks to someone doing the actual work, then superdumb things will happen. Then the info has to flow back the other way again. This is incredibly dumb.

Problems get solved quickly when a person just talks to a person in another department and makes the right thing happen. Anyone can and should talk to anyone else according to what they think is the fastest way to solve a problem for the benefit of the whole company. You can talk to your manager's manager without his permission. You can talk directly to a VP in another department. You can talk to me.

Communication should travel via the shortest path necessary to get the job done, not through the "chain of command."

> Any manager who attempts to enforce "chain of command" communication will soon find themselves working elsewhere.[283]
>
> You can talk to anyone without anyone else's permission. Moreover, you should consider yourself obligated to do so until the right thing happens.
>
> Always view yourself as working for the good of the company and never your department.[284]

How can it possibly help Tesla for departments to erect barriers between themselves or see their success as relative within the company instead of collective? We are all in the same boat.

Managers should work hard to ensure they are not creating silos within the company that create an us-versus-them mentality or impede communication in any way. This is a natural tendency and needs to be actively fought.[285]

The point is ensuring we execute ultrafast and well.[286]

Q: How do boundaries between departments affect product development?

You can see the organizational boundaries in the product. You'll often get a box in a box. You realize, "Why is this thing in two boxes?" Turns out, because both teams thought they needed an enclosure, the product ends up with an enclosure in an enclosure.

One case from the Tesla Model 3: The battery pack had a top enclosure and the car also has an underbody, right above it. What's the point of that? That doesn't make any sense, but because one team enclosed the battery pack and another team wanted to have an enclosed body, it happened.

It makes sense from an individual team's perspective, but you don't need a cover on the battery—there's a car on top of it. Putting the cover on the battery pack adds mass and cost, so it should be deleted.

Find the design necessity of every part and every process.[287]

Occasionally something seems necessary at the design level but turns out unnecessary in manufacturing. Connect designers and manufacturers to make sure they communicate often. The people on the assembly line should be able to immediately grab a designer or engineer and say, "WHY DID YOU MAKE IT THIS WAY!?'"

If your hand is on a stove and it gets hot, you pull it right off. But if it's someone else's hand on the stove, it will take you longer to do something about it.[288]

You cannot separate design, engineering, and manufacturing. They need to be together because you are going to make mistakes. You want to identify and fix those mistakes today, right now. And if you separate them, the mistakes will fester. Let the manufacturers put the designers' hands on the stove too.[289]

Whenever there are problems to solve, don't just meet with your managers. Do a skip level, where you meet with the level right below your managers.

> **Physically go to where the problem is, immediately.**[290]

One of my rules is "Go as close to the source as possible."

We were trying to determine how thick Starship's walls should be. Rather than only talking to the company's executives, I talked to some of the workers actually doing the welding. I asked what they thought was safe. The line workers thought the tank walls could get as thin as 4.8 millimeters.

"What about four?" I asked.

"That would make us pretty nervous," the workers replied.

"Okay," I said, "Let's try four millimeters."

It worked.[291]

SIMPLE COMMUNICATION

Don't use acronyms or nonsense words for objects, software, or processes. In general, anything that requires an explanation inhibits communication. We don't want people to have to memorize a glossary just to function.

I noticed a creeping tendency to use made-up acronyms at SpaceX and Tesla. Excessive use of made-up acronyms is a significant impediment to communication, and keeping communication clear as we grow is incredibly important.

A few acronyms here and there may not seem so bad, but if a thousand people are making these up, over time the result will be a huge glossary that we have to issue to new employees. No one actually remembers all these acronyms, and people don't want to seem dumb in a meeting, so they just sit there in ignorance.

I told people the acronyms needed to stop immediately or I would take drastic action. Unless an acronym is approved by me, it should not enter the SpaceX glossary. If there is an existing acronym that cannot reasonably be justified, it should be eliminated.

The key test for an acronym is to ask whether it helps or hurts communication. An acronym that most engineers outside of SpaceX already know, such as GUI (graphical user interface), is fine to use. It is also okay to use a few acronyms or contractions every now and again, assuming I have approved them. For example, we use MVac and M9 instead of Merlin 1C-Vacuum or Merlin 1C-Sea Level. But they need to be kept to a minimum.[292]

The most simple, straightforward, low-ego terms are generally best. You want to close the loop on reality hard.[293]

INNOVATION NEEDS PERMISSION TO FAIL

Failure is essentially irrelevant unless it is catastrophic.[294]

**FAILURE IS ESSENTIALLY IRRELEVANT
UNLESS IT IS CATASTROPHIC.**

You have to always look at the incentive structure of an organization and ask, "Is that organization properly incentivizing innovation?"[295] We're looking for any possible action that can improve the probability of success, no matter how small. Whether that comes from an intern, me, or anyone else doesn't matter.[296]

When trying new things, you've got to have some acceptance of failure...failure must be an option. If failure is not an option, it's going to result in extremely conservative choices and you may get something even worse than lack of innovation—things may go backward.[297]

When we had early failures in the SpaceX flights, I didn't fire anyone responsible for those particular causes of failure. They could have made better decisions, but they were smart and hardworking. It just wouldn't have been fair in that situation. Letting people go is only fair if they can't get themselves motivated around the core mission or they're really not giving it everything they can.[298]

It's important to create an environment that fosters innovation, and you want to let it evolve in a Darwinian way. You don't want to pick one technology or path and decide that it will win, because it may not be the best option. Let things evolve.[299]

With innovation and new technology, you don't know what the path is—there's no map. By nature it's unknown, which means you're going to make false moves. It must be culturally acceptable to make false moves.[300]

So to provide support for innovation, make sure the penalty for failure is low. You don't want the response to failure to be too punitive. That's one of the keys to Silicon Valley's success. There are many founders who've built successful companies after a previous company failed. They quickly reconstituted. People left and joined other companies. That's critical.[301]

If you punish people too much for failure, then they will respond accordingly, and the innovation you get will be incremental. Nobody's going to try anything bold for fear of getting fired or being punished in some way. If you expect innovation, the compensation structure must reflect that. The risk-reward must favor taking bold moves.[302]

Failure is a side effect of iteration. I once told a discouraged engineer, "If you can't tell me the four ways you fucked something up before you got it right, you weren't the one doing the real work."[303]

> If we're not occasionally blowing up an engine on the test stand, we're not trying hard enough.[304]

Q: Why is it so hard to predict what will work and what won't?

We do as much as we can on the ground and in simulations, but a lot of factors can't be simulated. A design might work in simulation or the test stand, but not in a real flight.[305] There's no test stand that can test a rocket at 17,000 mph, doing six Gs in every different orientation. It's not possible.[306]

After we fly a mission, hundreds of changes take place. Not a few. Hundreds. If you go to a detailed level across the ship, booster, and engines, there might be thousands of changes between flights. I'm just talking hardware here; software changes even more.[307]

Many are small, but a small change could be a big deal. The first issues you find are fundamental design flaws that would make success impossible. Some issues vary. They make success possible sometimes, but not every time. Maybe a design will blow up only once in a while. Things that work only sometimes can throw you off. Just because it worked once does not mean it will work again, because the combination of factors isn't the same. It requires a lot of flights to figure out which issues cause one in ten failures and which cause one in one hundred failures.[308]

> You will lose.
>
> It will hurt the first fifty times.
>
> When you get used to losing, you will play each game with less emotion.[309]

SIMPLICITY WINS

> Never use a cruise missile to kill a fly; just use a flyswatter.[310]

Every decision we made in early SpaceX designs has been with simplicity in mind. Simplicity both improves reliability and reduces cost. Fewer components means fewer components to buy and fewer components that can go wrong.[311]

The number of lines of code is not a figure of merit. I consider a large number of lines of code to be bad, not good. I would award one point for adding a line of code and two points for deleting a line of code.[312]

In general, always pick common sense as your guide. If following a "company rule" is obviously ridiculous in a particular situation, such that it would make for a great *Dilbert* cartoon, then the rule should change.[313]

> Simplicity is our mantra. It creates both reliability and low cost.[314]

Q: What are the benefits of simplicity at scale?

At Tesla, the Model 3 body line in Fremont was only ever meant to make five thousand cars a week, and it's now doing seven thousand. We achieved that by *removing* things. We had been doing a lot of foolish things. We've changed some of the designs and made them simpler and easier to build. Simplicity comes from hundreds of little changes.

Being able to get 40 percent more output from the same manufacturing line makes a big difference. It also reduces the marginal cost of production and improves the quality of the car. This is the result of a ton of hard work by a lot of people.[315]

For three months I was at the gigafactory trying to help fix battery production. It's a lot of little things. I look at every tiny part of each process and ask, "Is this process necessary?"

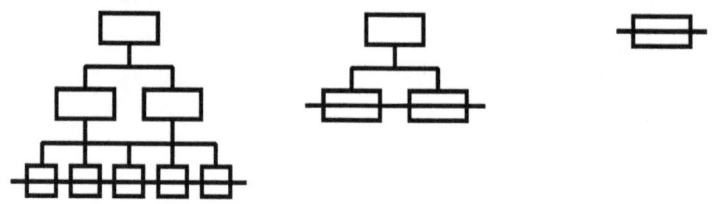

THE BEST PART IS NO PART.
THE BEST PROCESS IS NO PROCESS.

> The best part is no part. The best process is no process.[316]

For example, a robot would put a car frame on a turntable. The turntable would rotate and then another robot would pick it up. The problem was the turntable would sometimes break down. So, we eliminated the turntable. With a robot-to-robot handoff, we had one less step, less equipment, and didn't have turntable breakage to consider. It's a lot of this really simple stuff, but a thousand times.[317]

> It's a lot of minimizing things that can go wrong and maximizing the efficiency of the simple things.[318]

If you've got a whole bunch of separate parts and each of them has a given tolerance—even if that tolerance is tight, like 0.2 millimeter tolerance—but if you've got fifty parts...you have to multiply the variances together. You'll end up with a huge variance between cars. That's one of the reasons it's better to combine parts rather than have more individual parts.

In the Model 3 engineering, there were a lot of right answers to the wrong questions.[319]

Fifty different times for fifty different parts, an engineer would ask, "What's the best material to make this part out of?" Of course, they would get fifty different answers. They were all true individually, but not true collectively.

When you try to join all these parts made of dissimilar metals, there are many issues. You need better sealant to prevent galvanic corrosion. You've got to join some with rivets, some with spot welds, some with resin, or resin *and* spot welds. Then it looks like a Frankenstein situation all together.[320]

It's way better to have a single piece, casted. Then you have no gaps, no sealant, no dissimilar metals. You can reduce the size of the body shop in the factory dramatically. Having the rear body cast for Model Y allowed us to reduce the body shop by 30 percent.[321]

There's roughly a thousand robots on the Model 3 body line. Which, by the way, is not a figure of merit. We got rid of three hundred robots by switching to rear body casting. When we change the front body to casting, we'll get rid of another three hundred robots. You want fewer things, not more.[322]

It's easy to say "simplify," but it's very difficult to do it.[323]

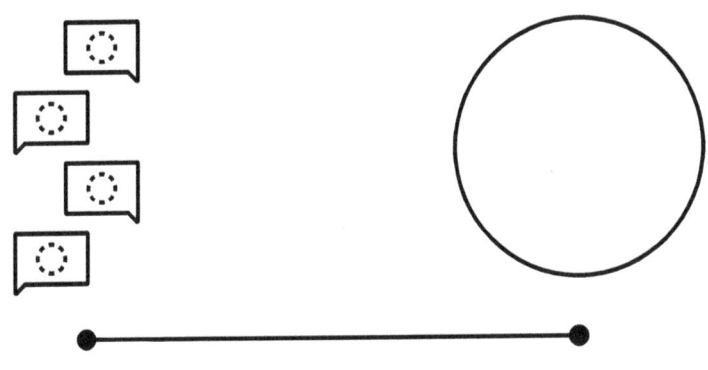

THE ALGORITHM

> I became a broken record on The Algorithm. But it's helpful to say it to an annoying degree.

I have everyone at my companies rigorously implement a five-step process for engineering. I call it The Algorithm. I'll list the steps, then explain. The order is very important.

1. Make your requirements less dumb.
2. Try very hard to delete the part or process.
3. Simplify or optimize.
4. Accelerate.
5. Automate.

Q: Why is the order of the steps so important?

> I've personally made the mistake of going backward—on all five steps—multiple times. Many things at Tesla were automated, accelerated, simplified, and then deleted.

One example was fiberglass mats on top of the battery pack. At one point I was basically living on the battery pack production line, because it was choking the entire car's production. The first mistake was trying to fix the automation to make the robot better, to make it move faster on a shorter path. We increased the rate by 20 percent, then 100 percent. Then, we tried to optimize the use of glue and the drying speed.

Automating was a mistake, then accelerating was a mistake, then optimizing was a mistake. Finally, I asked the battery safety team, "What the hell are these mats for? Fire protection?"

They said, "No, they're for noise and vibration."

I said, "But...you're the battery team."

So I asked the noise vibration analysis team, "What's the mat for?"

They said fire safety. It was like being in a *Dilbert* cartoon. I feel like I'm in a *Dilbert* cartoon quite frequently.

So we ran a test: a car with and without the fiberglass mats and a microphone in both. No one could tell the difference. So, we deleted the part (the mats), which deleted a step that required two million dollars of robotics, because it was just a big pile of nonsense.[324]

Q: Can you walk me through the steps?

The first step is to question the requirements, and make your requirements less dumb. You have to start there, because otherwise you could get the perfect answer to the wrong question. This step makes the question the least wrong possible.

Your requirements are definitely dumb. It does not matter who gave them to you. Requirements from smart people are the most dangerous, because you're less likely to question them. Always question requirements, even if it came from me. Everyone is wrong some of the time.

Whatever requirements or constraints you do have must come from a person, not a department. You can't actually ask a department. You have to be able to ask a person, and the person putting forth the requirement must take responsibility for that requirement. Otherwise, you could have a requirement made up by an intern two years ago off the cuff, or someone who isn't even at the company anymore. You must know the name of the real person who made every requirement.

Many times we've had dumb requirements, dug into them, and discovered no one currently working in that department agrees with the requirement. These things are often way more silly than you think. So step one is make your requirements less dumb.[325]

Step two: Try very hard to delete the part or process. It sounds obvious, but people often forget to try deleting something entirely.

IF YOU'RE NOT ADDING DELETED THINGS BACK IN 10% OF THE TIME, YOU'RE NOT DELETING ENOUGH.

If you're not adding deleted things back in 10 percent of the time, you're clearly not deleting enough. Somewhat illogically, people often feel they've succeeded if they are not forced to put anything back in. But actually they have failed in a different way, because they've been overly conservative and have left things in there that shouldn't be.

The bias tends to be very strong for adding this part or process step "just in case we need it." But you can make "just in case" arguments for many, many, many things.

People tend to remember, with sometimes a jarring level of pain, when they deleted something they later needed. They overcorrect, and put too much stuff in there, which overcomplicates things.

I tell them this in advance: "Look, we're deliberately going to delete more than we should. Some of the things we delete, we're going to put back in. At least one in ten things, we're going to add back in." People get a little shook by that. But if you're so conservative in deleting that you never have to put anything back in, you obviously have a lot of stuff that isn't needed. So, you've got to overcorrect for that tendency.

At SpaceX, I would tell the team, "We are on a deletion *rampage*!! Nothing is sacred. We will delete any remotely questionable tubes, sensors, manifolds, etc. tonight. Please go ultrahardcore on deletion and simplification." We put immense effort into reducing mass.

There's a recursive factor to mass. If you add an extra ton of heat shielding, you also need more fuel to get it to orbit, and you need more fuel to deorbit, and you need more fuel to land it. Also the structure now has more load on it, because it's carrying an extra ton of heat shield. This applies to any given ton.

Adding each ton is almost like adding two tons when it's fully considered. We've calculated it to be around a 1.8 recursion factor, but we're probably forgetting something that gets us closer to two. Every one ton of mass begets an extra ton. That is why it is very important to delete.[326]

Recapping so far: Step one, make your requirements less dumb. Step two, try hard to delete the part or process.[327]

Then, once you have deleted as much as you can, the *third* step is to simplify or optimize. The third step. The *third* step. *Not* the first step. Why?

> The most common mistake of smart engineers is to optimize a thing that should not exist.

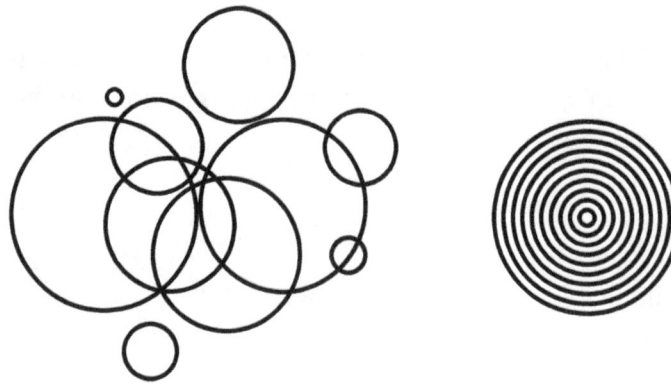

THE MOST COMMON MISTAKE OF SMART ENGINEERS
IS TO OPTIMIZE A THING THAT SHOULD NOT EXIST.

Everyone was trained in high school and college to answer the question in front of them. It's convergent logic. You can't tell the professor, "Your question is dumb." You have to answer the question. Without knowing it, almost everyone has this mental straightjacket on. They'll work on optimizing a thing that should simply not exist.

Then, and only then, step four: accelerate cycle time. Once you're moving in the right direction, and moving efficiently... you're moving too slow. Go faster. You can always make things go faster.

But, do *not* go faster until you have worked on the other three things first. I mistakenly spent a lot of time accelerating processes that I later realized should have been deleted. Speeding up something that shouldn't exist is absurd. If you're digging your grave, don't dig it faster. Stop digging.

Step five, the final step, is to automate. The big mistake I made in the Tesla factories in Nevada and Fremont was trying to automate every step too early. To fix that, we had to tear hundreds of expensive robots out of the production line. We put a hole in the side of the building just to remove all that equipment.[328]

Always wait until the end of designing a process—after you have questioned all the requirements and deleted unnecessary parts—before you introduce automation.[329]

MANIACAL URGENCY

A maniacal sense of urgency is our operating principle.[330]

DON'T WASTE TIME

Excessive meetings are the blight of big companies and almost always get worse over time. Get rid of all large meetings, unless you're certain they are providing value to the whole audience, in which case, keep them short.

Also get rid of frequent meetings, unless you are dealing with an extremely urgent matter. Meeting frequency should drop rapidly once the urgent matter is resolved.

Walk out of a meeting or drop off a call as soon as it is obvious you aren't adding value. It is not rude to leave; it is rude to make someone stay and waste their time.

SPEED IS BOTH OFFENSE AND DEFENSE

> The only true currency is time.[331]

The best offense and defense is speed. The SR-71 Blackbird is a military plane with almost no defense except acceleration. It was never shot down. Not even once. Over three thousand missiles were shot at the SR-71 Blackbird and none hit. All it did was go faster. The power of speed is underappreciated as a competitive factor.[332]

The real way you actually achieve intellectual property (IP) protection is by innovating fast. If your rate of innovation is high, then you don't need to worry about protecting the IP because other companies will be copying something you did years ago. That's fine. Just make sure your rate of innovation is fast. Speed of innovation is what matters.[333]

We obviously cannot compete with the big car companies in size, so we must do so with intelligence and agility.[334] A factory moving at twice the speed of another factory is basically equivalent to two factories. The company will succeed if it can do with one factory what takes other companies two, three, or four factories. We try to think, "How can we make each factory produce what would normally require five or even ten factories?"[335]

> I have a running triage of what I do at each company, constantly thinking, "What is the most useful thing I could do?"[336]

In early SpaceX, I told the team everything we did was a function of our burn rate. We were burning through a hundred thousand dollars per day. In the same way, I expected the revenue in ten years to be ten million dollars a day. Every day we were slower to achieve our goals was a day of missing out on that revenue.[337]

You need to be a vector, not just a scalar. That means you need to go at high speed *in the right direction*. No company will *always* be going in the right direction all the time—so you have to do course corrections, like a guided missile.[338]

I try to work as much as possible—to the edge of sanity. Every good hour or even minute of thinking about Tesla and SpaceX has such a big effect on the company. It makes sleeping difficult.

Tesla is getting to the point where every high-quality minute of thinking has a million-dollar impact. That is insane. If Tesla is doing $2 billion a week in revenue, that's about $300 million a day, seven days a week. There are many instances where a half-hour meeting improved the company's financial outcome by $100 million.[339]

DO THINGS IN PARALLEL

Everything is measured in terms of time. What is the time risk associated with something?

The one thing you cannot replace is time.[340]

```
00:10
00:09
00:08
00:07
00:06
00:05
00:04
00:03
00:02
00:01
```

THE ONE THING YOU CANNOT REPLACE IS TIME.

For PayPal, we needed to establish a lot of back-office relationships to attach various data sources. The credit card system for processing credit cards, the Federal Reserve System for doing electronic funds transfers, the various fraud databases to run fraud checks. There was a lot we had to interface with, and it took a while to set all that up.

But by doing them all in parallel, it all came together simultaneously. Developing the software and having it ready for the general public coincided with us concluding deals with the outside vendors. All that took about a year.[341]

Avoid serialized dependencies. A lot of things have a "gestation period" and there is nothing you can do to accelerate it. If you can have all those things gestating in parallel, that will substantially accelerate your overall timeline. People tend to serialize too much. Put as many gestating elements in parallel as possible.[342]

If a timeline is long, it's wrong.[343]

BREAK DOWN THE "IMPOSSIBLE"

The general principles of first-principle thinking apply to software, hardware, anything really. Often, we were told something was impossible, but once we broke it down into its constituent elements, we could solve those.[344]

For xAI in 2024, we were trying to build a training supercluster (a giant network of computers to train an AI model). We went to the various suppliers and said we needed one hundred thousand H100s (superpowerful computer chips) to be able to train coherently. Their estimates for how long it would take to complete that were eighteen to twenty-four months. Well, we needed to get that done in six months or we wouldn't be competitive.

So, we broke that down. We need a building; we need power; we need cooling.

We didn't have enough time to build a building from scratch. So, we found a factory in Memphis that was no longer in use. The input power was 15 megawatts and we needed 150 megawatts. So, we rented generators and put them along one side of the building.

Then, we needed cooling. So, we rented about a quarter of the mobile cooling capacity of the US and put the chillers on the other side of the building.

That didn't fully solve the problem because the power variations during training are very big. Power can drop by 50 percent in 100 milliseconds, which the generators can't keep up with. So then we added Tesla megapacks and modified the software in the megapacks to be able to smooth out the power variation during the training run.

Then there were a bunch of networking challenges. Networking cables for one hundred thousand GPUs (graphics processing units) are very, very difficult. We ran the networking team to do the cabling in four shifts, 24/7. I was sleeping in the data center and doing cabling myself.[345]

Now called Colossus, it is currently the largest AI training platform in the world. It was constructed in 122 days. Ninety-two days later, it had been doubled to two hundred thousand GPUs.[346]

SET AGGRESSIVE TIMELINES

> I often tell the Tesla team: "It's okay to scrap equipment or money. It's not okay to scrap time."[347]

When I was interviewing for a vice president of machining, I explained I was paying for everything at SpaceX out of pocket. I asked him, "What's the cheapest you would work for?" He haggled, and eventually we agreed. Ten minutes later, I gave him a contract. This was a Saturday at 5:00 p.m. He started working that night.[348]

Q: Do you deliberately make aggressive prediction timelines to drive people to be ambitious?

For internal timelines, we set the most aggressive timelines we can. I do this because there's a kind of "law of gaseous expansion" for schedules. Whatever time you set, it's not going to be less than that. It's rare that something will ever get done faster than the schedule.[349]

When I cite a schedule, it is actually the schedule I think is true. It's not some fake schedule I made up. It may be delusional—that is entirely possible, and that has happened from time to time. But it's never some knowingly fake deadline, ever.[350]

I want to emphasize that some dates are not dates that will actually be met. For example, the initial release date for the Model 3 at Tesla was an impossible date because there are seven thousand unique components in the Model 3, and our deadline assumed all of them would arrive on time. That won't happen. But, it was a date for us to hold ourselves (internally) and our suppliers to.[351]

> I do have a habit of being optimistic with schedules.[352]

When I give estimates about our production, it's guesswork. Especially guesses about exponential curves. In exponential growth, the difference a year or two makes to an outcome is enormous. We got a lot of criticism for the number of cars we delivered in 2017. The area under the curve of production in 2017 was quite small because it was the beginning of an exponential ramp, but once that growth got going, the area under the curve was enormous. That's why people were so shocked. I kept trying to say this, but people don't understand what exponential means.[353]

In 2018, we doubled our global fleet, cumulatively. We made and delivered about as many cars as we had in our entire history. Most people thought it wasn't possible. If you predicted linear growth, it wouldn't seem possible.

But when making estimates involving exponential growth, small changes in the calendar breakpoint have enormous percentage differences in outcome. The time difference is small, but the percentage difference in the outcome is enormous.[354]

As far as our predictions are concerned, the media tends to report all the wrong ones and ignore all the correct ones. I've had a long career in multiple industries. If you list just my sins, I sound like the worst person on Earth. But if you put those in the context of what I've done right, it makes much more sense.

> I don't want to blow your mind, but I'm not always right.[355]

The longer you do anything, the more mistakes you will make, cumulatively. If you sum up just the mistakes, it sounds like I'm the worst predictor ever, which is not the case.

Some of them happen sooner or later, but they do tend to come true. It's rare they do not come true eventually. For radical technology predictions, the point is not that it was a few years late, but that it happened at all. That's the more important part.[356]

> I may be a little optimistic, but I always deliver.[357]

WE MUST MAKE STUFF

Manufacturing is underrated. It's hard.[358]

THE REAL WORK

> Some people have an absurd view of the economy as a magic thing that just produces stuff.

They think goods and services magically come from somewhere, and if somebody has more stuff than somebody else, it's because they took more from this magic source of stuff.[359]

Now, let me break it to the fools out there. If we don't make stuff, there's no stuff. If we don't grow the food, process the food, and transport the food...there's no food. Medical treatments, getting your teeth fixed, everything. There's no stuff if we don't make stuff.

Some people have become detached from reality. This notion that the government can just send checks out to everybody and everything will be fine is not true—*obviously*. You can't just legislate money to solve things. If you don't make stuff, there is no stuff. The whole machine could grind to a halt.[360]

Technological progress is not inevitable. It's not some kind of abstract concept. Humans make technology. If we don't do it, it will not happen.[361]

> Somebody has to do the real work.

There's an overallocation of talent in finance and law, especially in the United States. Too many smart people go into finance and law. This is both a compliment and a criticism. We should have fewer people doing law and finance and more people making stuff.

Manufacturing used to be highly valued in the United States. These days it hasn't been as much, which I think is wrong. Making cars is an honest day's living, that's for sure. Making anything or providing a valuable service like good entertainment, good information—these are valuable things to do.[362]

> I've got mad respect for the makers of things.[363]

THE FACTORY IS THE PRODUCT

> The biggest epiphany I had building Tesla is what really matters is the machine that builds the machines—the factory.[364]

To accelerate a sustainable future, Tesla had to scale up production volume as quickly as possible. That is why Tesla engineering transitioned to focus heavily on designing the machine that makes the machines—turning the factory itself into the product.

A first-principles physics analysis of automotive production suggests that somewhere between a fivefold to tenfold improvement is achievable by version three on a roughly two-year iteration cycle.[365]

Tesla believes strongly in making things. Apple and Google do not. It's a philosophical difference. We believe that manufacturing technology is itself subject to a tremendous amount of innovation. In fact, we believe there's more potential for innovation in manufacturing than in the design of a car—by a long shot. This is just a philosophical difference. Perhaps we are wrong. But we believe in manufacturing, and a company that values manufacturing as highly as we do will attract the best minds in manufacturing.[366]

> Our success or failure will not be because of competition. It will be our capability to make a high-quality product at a price people can afford.[367]

You've got this giant factory, a cybernetic collective with ten thousand things going wrong and you've got to solve them all. Fast. If you don't solve problems fast enough, the factory doesn't go. A big factory burns a huge amount of money every minute you aren't making a product.[368]

ATTACK THE CONSTRAINT

> Designing a rocket is trivial.

There are tons of books you can read, and if you can understand equations, you can design a rocket. Real easy. But making even one of these things and getting it to orbit is very hard.[369]

It's the same thing for cars. It's easy to make a car prototype; it's hard to do car production.[370]

This is underappreciated. People think there is a "eureka" moment where you come up with an idea and that's it. They believe design is the hard part and production is just making copies. That's completely false.[371]

At Tesla, we learned a valuable lesson. The production line will move as fast as the slowest and least lucky part of the entire production line. Let's say there are ten thousand things that have to go right for production to work. If you have 9,999 things working and one that isn't, that sets the production rate.[372]

Things move as fast as the least lucky or least competent supplier. Any natural disaster you care to name has happened to our suppliers. A supplier had a factory burn down. An earthquake. A tsunami. Massive hail. A tornado. A ship sank. A shoot-out at the Mexican border. I'm not kidding. That delayed trunk carpet.[373]

So when scaling SpaceX, we spent ten to one hundred times more effort on designing the manufacturing system than on designing the Raptor engine.³⁷⁴ We built the rockets first and the factory later, because building the production system is the harder thing.³⁷⁵

Design is overrated, and manufacturing is underrated. There is 1,000 percent, maybe 10,000 percent more work that goes into the production system than the product itself.³⁷⁶ Especially for a product with new technology. The difficulty of manufacturing is proportionate to the amount of new technology in the product.³⁷⁷

MANUFACTURING IS THE MOAT

Two things define manufacturing competitiveness: economies of scale and technology. If you maximize your level of technology and maximize your level of scale, this is obviously going to be the most competitive situation. That's why plants are so freaking giant.[378]

Our plant in Texas starts from actual rail cars of raw materials coming in. We form the battery cell and the battery pack, build the motor, and cast the parts. We also have introduced a major innovation, which is to cast the entire front third and rear third of the car as a single piece. I got this idea from toy cars.

I wondered, "Toys are cheap! How do they make toys?"

"They just cast them."

I was like, "Well, can you build a casting machine big enough for a car?"

They said, "No one ever has."

"Are we breaking any laws of physics?"

"No..."

"Well, let's just ask them."

There were six major casting machine suppliers in the world at the time. Five of them said no and the sixth said maybe. I said, "I'll take that as a yes."[379]

Prototypes are easy and fun. Reaching volume production with a reliable product at an affordable price is excruciatingly difficult.[380]

PART III

BUILDING COMPANIES

Q: What fuels your creativity?

Pressure. Necessity.[381]

BECOMING A FOUNDER

> You want to embark on something where success is certain to be one of the possible outcomes.[382]

Q: What was the path to starting your first company?

Growing up in South Africa, it seemed like a lot of the advanced technology was being produced in America and Silicon Valley, especially. I wanted to go where I could be involved in the creation of new technology. That's what took me first to Canada (because I could get citizenship in Canada through my mom) and then ultimately to the US.[383]

When I was seventeen, I got my Canadian passport. Three weeks later I was in Canada.[384] I left South Africa and landed in Montreal. I arrived with a backpack, a suitcase of books, and $2,000.

I stayed in a youth hostel for a few days, then bought a bus ticket for one hundred bucks to go across the country, making stops along the way.[385]

I managed to get to Swift Current in Saskatchewan. My cousin's son had a wheat farm where I worked for about six weeks, as I turned eighteen. We did a barn raising, cleared out the wheat bins and grain silos, and worked the vegetable patch.[386]

Then I got back on the bus and went to Vancouver. I had a half-uncle there in the lumber industry. I ended up working at a lumber mill chainsawing logs and cleaning out the pulp boiler. That might be the hardest job I've had. You had to crawl through this little tunnel in a hazmat suit and then shovel this steaming sand and mush out of the boilers to clean them out. There's only one entrance or exit, a little tunnel. If you're claustrophobic, it would be real bad. It did not seem safe. But it was the highest-paying job at the employment office. Other jobs were under eight dollars an hour, and this one was eighteen dollars an hour.[387]

I worked there as a lumberjack doing odd jobs for a few months. Then I applied for college, and went to Queen's University in Kingston. I was there for a couple years before applying to UPenn. I didn't think I'd be able to go because I was paying my own way through university. That's not too hard in Canada because tuition is highly subsidized, but in the US college is more expensive.[388]

> I paid my own way through college and dropped out of Stanford grad school with $110K in college debt.[389]

Physics and computer science were always my two best subjects, because I wanted to figure out the nature of the universe. I thought I might do physics at a particle accelerator, banging particles together to see what happens in a research facility. Then, the supercollider got canceled in the US, and I realized I could study for years to work at a collider, and then the government could arbitrarily cancel it. Decision made: I could not do that.[390]

Q: How did you decide to leave your PhD program and start your first company?

Because of my interest in electric cars as a college student, I took an internship at a company that made high-energy-density capacitors. My intent was to get a PhD in energy storage solutions for electric vehicles. I was going to Stanford to study material science and the physics of high-energy-density capacitors for use in electric vehicles.[391]

But, I wasn't sure if my work during that PhD would actually be useful. I was concerned it could be academically useful but not practically useful.[392]

Success on an academic level would have been quite likely. I could publish a paper, but most papers are pretty useless.[393] Once in a while you get something spectacular but it's pretty rare.[394] How many PhD papers are actually used by someone, ever? Percentagewise, not many. You add a leaf to the tree of knowledge, but that leaf could be saying, *Nope, not possible. This is not good enough technology to be used in an electric vehicle.* There goes seven years of my life.[395]

Not that I cared about the PhD, actually. I just needed a lab. I could spend years working in a lab and maybe the technology would work...or maybe it wouldn't.[396]

> I was not sure success was even a possibility. I thought maybe it was, but I wasn't sure.[397]

Then the internet started taking off. It was clear to me the internet was happening in 1995, although most people weren't aware of it then.[398] I was pretty sure success was one of the possible outcomes for an internet company. I knew watching the internet get built while doing a PhD would be frustrating.[399] I decided to put graduate school on hold and start an internet company.[400]

I thought I'd be able to come back to electric vehicles. I figured electric vehicle technology and energy storage technology would have a natural progression, and that ended up happening.

In 1995, it was not obvious you could make any money on the internet. Until Netscape went public in late 1995, nobody thought you could make a valuable internet company. Now it seems obvious. But back then, it was not at all.

Humanity was effectively becoming a superorganism, qualitatively different from what it had been before. I wanted to be part of that. I wanted to help build humanity's nervous system.[401]

The internet turned out to be a good idea for my first company because software is a low-capital endeavor. I didn't have any money, and had a bunch of student debt. You don't need a lot of tooling and equipment to get started. Software you can just write by yourself. It's not capital intensive. Starting something software-related as your first company is much, much easier.[402]

STARTING ZIP2

> When we first started Zip2, our ambitions were quite low: make enough money to pay rent.[403]

Q: When did you start your first company?

Starting a company was not actually the first thing I tried. I tried to get a job at Netscape, but they didn't reply to my emails. So I went to hang out in the lobby at Netscape. I didn't know who to talk to, and I was too shy to talk to anyone. I figured, "If I can't get a job, I'll just try writing my own software."[404]

It wasn't actually from the desire to start a company. I just wanted to be part of building the internet in some way. Since I couldn't get a job at an internet company, I had to start one myself.[405]

I wanted to try to build something useful, but I didn't think I would build anything particularly great. Probabilistically, greatness seemed unlikely, but I wanted to at least try.[406]

We started off building maps, directions, and classified ads. It was, to the best of my knowledge, the first map and directions on the internet. There may still be some patents—or maybe they lapsed at this point. (Note from Eric: there is, patent #5944769.[407]) The whole initial code base I wrote myself because there wasn't anyone else. It was just me.[408]

I was twenty-four at the time and only had a few thousand dollars saved. I convinced my brother to join, and he brought about five thousand dollars, which was a lot for us. For the first few months, we only had one computer. When the website wasn't working, it was because I was compiling code. The website was up during the day; I was coding at night, seven days a week, all the time. We more or less squatted in the office because the landlord was always out of the country, and nobody was using it.[409]

Soon, there were six of us. Me, my brother, a friend of my mom's, and three salespeople we hired on contingency by putting an ad in the newspaper.[410]

Things were pretty tough in the early going. I didn't have any money. In fact, I had negative money because of a huge student debt. I couldn't afford an apartment and an office, so I rented an office because that was cheaper. I slept on the futon at the office and showered at the YMCA. I briefly had a girlfriend in that period and to stay with me, she had to sleep in the office. I was in the best shape—every day a workout, shower, and you're good to go![411]

There was a small internet service provider on the floor below us, so we drilled a hole through the floor and connected a modem cable. That got us our internet connection for one hundred bucks a month. We had a tiny revenue stream, but an absurdly tiny burn rate. We actually had more revenue than we had expenses. When we talked to VCs (venture capitalists), we could say we were profitable.[412]

> Most venture capitalists wouldn't take a meeting with us, though.
>
> They said, "Who's made money on the internet? No one. Okay, pass."[413]

There was a lot more interest in the internet following the Netscape IPO (initial public offering). Our software was more impressive by then, too. Mohr Davidow Ventures (a VC firm) invested $3 million for 60 percent of the company, which we thought was crazy. They're going to give us money for nothing? They must be mad. It seemed insane to give us so much money for a company that consisted of six people at the time. But it worked out well for them.[414]

Q: How did the original idea for Zip2 come about?

We needed to build something that would earn money quickly. We thought the media industry would need help converting their content from print to electronic, and they clearly had money. If we could help them move to the internet, maybe we could generate revenue. There was no advertising revenue on the internet at the time. That was the basis of Zip2.[415]

We hired a lot more people and wrote software to bring newspapers online. Knight Ridder, New York Times Company, and Hearst all became investors and customers. And at one point, Zip2 was responsible for a significant section of the New York Times Company website. I got to know the media industry well.[416]

The challenge was too much control by the existing media companies. They had too many board seats and too much voting control over Zip2. They kept trying to push the company in directions that made no sense. We actually had good software—comparable to Yahoo! or Excite at the time. It was all being forced through media companies, who would not fully use it. We built the best technology, but it wasn't being deployed properly.[417]

> It's a bit like building F-22 fighter jets and selling them to people who roll them down the hill at each other. Not the way to use the technology![418]

That's when I realized you want to sell your products straight to the end consumer. If you've got great technology, go directly to the end consumer. Don't sell it to some bonehead legacy company that doesn't understand how to use it.[419]

Fortunately, Compaq came along.[420] We had the opportunity to sell Zip2 to Compaq in early 1999 and accepted that offer. It was a little over $300 million in cash. Cash is a currency I highly recommend.[421]

To this day, that moment astonishes me. At the time I was living in a house with four housemates. Literally, a check came in my mailbox. I was like, "This is insane. What if somebody…? I mean, I guess they'd have trouble cashing it?" Seems like a weird way to send money. My bank account went from $5,000 to $21,005,000.[422]

Immediately after the sale, I didn't take any time off. I still had to pay taxes, then I ended up putting almost all of that into X.com (which became PayPal). This was early 1999, and there were a lot of opportunities remaining on the internet.[423]

I've always wanted to push my chips back on the table or play the next level of the game. I'm not good at sitting back.[424]

GOING ALL IN, AGAIN (ZIP2 EARNINGS INTO PAYPAL)

It was frustrating.

We built incredible technology at Zip2, and it had not been used. I wanted to build another internet company to show technology can be extremely effective when used properly.[425]

I felt like we had our wings clipped somewhat with Zip2. I wanted to avoid being constrained by our customers like that, and go direct-to-consumer. That's what motivated me to start PayPal.[426]

Q: How did you come up with the idea for PayPal?

I thought, *What was essentially digital? What exists in the form of information, but is not high bandwidth?* In 1999, most people still had modems, so video was not really feasible. Money is low bandwidth and mostly digital. What can we do to make money work better?[427]

Money is like a database for guiding people to decide what they should do. You can think of banks as a set of databases.[428]

The 1990s financial infrastructure was a bunch of ancient mainframes, running ancient code, doing batch processing with poor security, and a series of heterogeneous databases. A herky-jerky frickin' monstrosity.

From an information theory standpoint, finance would be much better if it could be real-time, secure, and fast. Essentially just one real-time database. Let's try to build that.

Q: Can you explain the PayPal idea from an information theory perspective?

Think of money as information. People often think money has power in and of itself. It does not. Money is just information. Money is a database for resource allocation across time and space.

Let's try thinking in the limit, as I explained before. If you are stranded on a tropical island with a trillion dollars, it's useless. On the island there are no resources to allocate, except yourself, so money doesn't help. If you're stranded with no food, all the Bitcoin in the world will not stop you from starving.

You need something to create ratios of value between products and services. In an economy, you have a massive number of products and services. You can't trade for everything. That would be extremely unwieldy. You need something to create the ratio of exchange between goods and services. You also need something that allows us to shift obligations across time, like debt and equity.[429]

The quality of money as a system is a function of different variables. Just like an internet connection, you want high bandwidth, low latency, and few errors.[430]

What PayPal really did was help improve the bandwidth—the speed at which money could move. Instead of mailing checks back and forth, you could do real-time exchange of money online. Sellers could then ship items immediately instead of waiting for a check and then for the bank to clear it.⁴³¹

> We should look at currencies from an information theory standpoint.
>
> Whichever has least error and latency will win.

That's what X.com originally was. I thought we should try to do all the financial things as well—not just payments. I still think that's what PayPal should have done, but whatever. It's water under the bridge at this point.⁴³²

I rolled most of my Zip2 money into X.com, investing $12.5 million.⁴³³ In 1999, Sequoia invested in X.com, buying $5 million in shares, and Mike Moritz joined the company's board. When Moritz invested, he said we should hire a CEO. I said, "Great, I don't want to be CEO." I had no desire to be a CEO. It's a lot of chores…being CEO sucks. He also told me, "Dude, you should not invest basically everything except your house and car in your startup."⁴³⁴

> I kept the chips on the table.⁴³⁵

LISTEN WELL, CORRECT FAST

The initial thought with X.com was to create a conglomeration of financial services, so you have one place where all your financial service needs could be seamlessly integrated and work smoothly.

We had a little feature: payments through email. When we showed the system to someone, we'd show the hard part first: the conglomeration of financial services. Nobody was interested.

Then we showed people email payments, which were relatively easy to build, and everybody was interested. So, we focused on email payments. That's what really got PayPal to take off.

It's important to take feedback from your environment. If we hadn't responded to what people said, we probably would not have been successful. It's important to look for things like that, focus on them, and correct your prior assumptions. You want to close those loops as quickly and clearly as possible.[436]

I'm trying to create an accurate mental model of reality. If I have a wrong view on something, or if there's a nuanced improvement that can be made, I say, "I used to think this, which turned out to be wrong—thank goodness I don't have that wrong belief anymore."[437]

I'm a huge believer in taking feedback.

We took a similar approach with PayPal that worked at Zip2, which was to have a small group of very talented people, and keep it small. PayPal had maybe thirty engineers for a system which I would say is more sophisticated than the Federal Reserve clearing system.

Both Zip2 and PayPal operated like Silicon Valley startups. Pretty flat hierarchy, everybody had a similar desk, and anyone could talk to anyone.

We had a philosophy of "best idea wins" as opposed to the person proposing the idea winning because of who they are. Even though there were times when I thought that should have been the way to go. Everyone was an equity stakeholder.[438]

If there were two options, and one wasn't obviously better than the other, rather than spend time trying to pick which one was slightly better, we would just pick one and go. Sometimes we were wrong and picked the suboptimal path, but at least we moved fast.[439]

> Better to pick a path and keep moving than just vacillate endlessly on a decision.

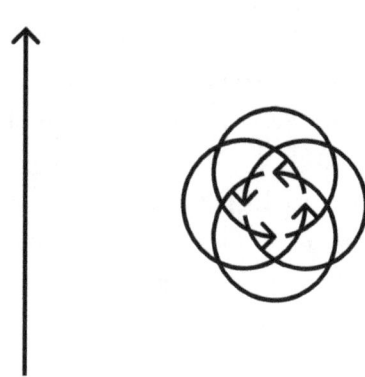

BETTER TO PICK A PATH AND KEEP MOVING THAN
JUST VACILLATE ENDLESSLY ON A DECISION.

We were focused on building the best product we possibly could. Both Zip2 and PayPal were product-focused companies. We didn't worry too much about intellectual property paperwork. We were incredibly obsessive about building the best possible customer experience. That was a far more effective selling tool than having a giant sales force or marketing gimmicks.[440]

Pay close attention to negative feedback, and solicit it, particularly from friends. It's incredibly helpful.

This may sound like simple advice, but hardly anyone does it.[441]

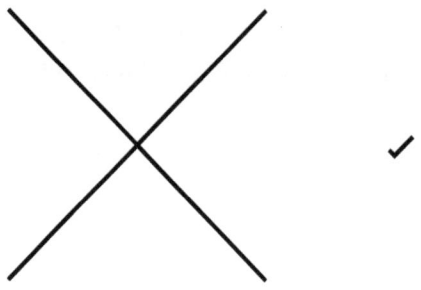

**PAY CLOSE ATTENTION TO NEGATIVE FEEDBACK,
AND SOLICIT IT, PARTICULARLY FROM FRIENDS.
IT'S INCREDIBLY HELPFUL.**

UNITE AND CONQUER

> What matters to me is winning, and not in a small way.[442]

Around the same time I was starting X, another company formed called Confinity, which was Peter Thiel, Max Levchin, Luke Nosek, David Sacks, Ken Howery, etc. At X.com, we had Jeremy Stoppelman, who created Yelp, and Roelof Botha, who went on to run Sequoia. Both companies had a crazy amount of talent.

Confinity started as a PalmPilot cryptography company, back when you could communicate through the infrared port of a PalmPilot. Then they evolved in the direction of payments as well. We were both in Palo Alto, a block away from each other—at one point, even in the same building. We were competing with each other like maniacs.

Finally, we had coffee on University Avenue and said, "Hey, why don't we just combine our efforts? Otherwise we're gonna bludgeon each other to death." We knew we had to get that deal done fast or we were both gonna die.

So we merged Confinity with X.com and raised $100 million in three weeks during March of 2000.[443] About a year later, we changed the company name to the product name, PayPal.[444]

> We went from starting a company to fourteen months later merging and having a valuation of $500 million in March of 2000. It felt so sudden, like, "This is completely ridiculous."[445]

In April 2000, the market went into freefall.[446] The challenge was keeping the company alive for the next two years.[447]

There was a lot of drama; it was a turbulent period. I didn't expect PayPal's growth rate to be what it was, and that created major problems. After the first month of the website being active, we had one hundred thousand customers. It was nutty.[448] We definitely did not anticipate that.[449]

Q: What made PayPal's growth rate so dramatic?

PayPal was a perfect case for viral marketing. Like Hotmail, one customer would be like a salesperson for you, bringing other customers. Customers would send money to a friend and bring that friend into the network. We had this exponential growth, where the more customers we had, the faster it grew. It was like bacteria in a petri dish, following an S-curve.[450]

We started off first by offering people twenty dollars if they opened an account and twenty dollars if they referred anyone. Then we dropped it to ten dollars. Then we dropped it to five dollars. As the network got bigger and bigger, the value of the network itself exceeded any sort of carrot that we could offer.[451] We probably spent $60 or $70 million in incentives to build that network. That seems like a lot, but it built a very valuable network. The relative cost depends on your scale. That's a peanut to Google.[452]

Q: Leading through that kind of growth seems very challenging. How did you manage it all?

I ran PayPal for about the first two years of its existence. We launched after year one, and by the end of year two we had a million customers. It gives you a sense for how fast things can grow. We didn't have a sales force, VP of sales, or VP of marketing and we didn't spend any money on advertising.[453]

It wasn't easy, because we still had some bugs in the software. Even if the bug only occurs one in one thousand times, that's still a thousand *angry* customers shouting, "Where is my money!?"

We had a customer service office on University Avenue in Palo Alto with five people. When something went wrong, customer service phones would explode. We had many challenges. Various financial regulatory agencies were trying to shut us down. The FTC was trying to shut us down. Visa, MasterCard, and eBay were all trying to have us shut down. There were a lot of battles.[454]

> It was a close call. We came close to dying in 2000 and 2001.[455]

FROM EXILE TO EXIT

> I was away for two weeks and the management team decided I wasn't the right guy to run the company.
>
> Instead of fighting during a critical time, I thought it was best to concede.[456]

It's not a good idea to leave the office when there are a lot of major things underway that are causing people a great deal of stress. I left for a trip, a combination of needing to raise money and I had gotten married earlier that year and had not had a vacation or honeymoon. It was kind of a combined financing trip and honeymoon. Also not a great idea.

I got removed as CEO of PayPal because I wanted to do a bunch of things that seemed extremely risky. I think they would have worked out, but at a time when companies were dropping like flies, I was proposing we do all these things that sound risky—it was much too scary for the rest of the team.[457]

I didn't agree with their conclusion, but I understood why they took the action they did. Peter, Max, David, and the other guys are smart people with the right motivations. They did what they thought was right, for the right reasons. The reasons weren't valid in my opinion but it's hard to argue with the ultimate outcome, which was positive.

It would be easy to be bitter and hate them forever, but the better course of action is to turn the other cheek. I put a lot of effort into making things good between us, and they became good. I invested in some of Peter's companies, including Founders Fund, which is made up primarily of former PayPal people. Peter, who replaced me as CEO, later invested in SpaceX.[458]

Life is too short for long-term grudges.[459]

Q: What was the exit like?

In about February of 2002, PayPal went public. I think we were the only internet company to go public in the first part of 2002. It went reasonably well, although I can imagine we set a record on SEC rewrites. This was right around the time of Enron and other corporate scandals, so they put us through the wringer.[460]

It was a tough, long-running battle between PayPal and eBay's payment system, and it was certainly challenging. There were times it felt like trying to win a land war in Asia. They got to set the ground rules. It was like trying to beat Microsoft inside their own operating system. It took a lot of effort to beat eBay in their own system. One of the long-term risks for PayPal was eBay would one day prevail. One way to retire that risk was to sell to eBay.[461]

In October 2002, we struck a deal to sell PayPal to eBay for about $4.5 billion.[462]

I could go and buy one of the islands of the Bahamas and turn it into my personal fiefdom, but I am much more interested in trying to build and create a new company.

I haven't spent my winnings.

I'm going to put almost all of it back into a new game.[463]

BUILDING TESLA

Accelerating the removal of hydrocarbons from the crust and placing them in the atmosphere is unwise. This is one of the biggest problems of the twenty-first century.

Hopefully this transition to sustainable energy occurs before it's too late.[464]

THE MISSION TO PROTECT THE PLANET

> There's no way we can conserve our way to a good future. We have to make energy sustainable.[465]

Q: Why is the mission of Tesla so important to you?

The overarching purpose of Tesla is to help expedite the move from a mine-and-burn hydrocarbon economy toward a solar-electric economy, which I believe to be the primary, but not exclusive, sustainable solution.[466]

Energy output is the foundation of the economy, just like sunlight is the foundation of the ecosystem. To a first approximation, a country's goods and services production will be proportionate to its energy output.[467]

By definition, we must at some point achieve a sustainable energy economy or we will run out of fossil fuels to burn and civilization will collapse. Given that we *must* get off fossil fuels anyway, and that *virtually all* scientists agree dramatically increasing atmospheric and oceanic carbon levels is insane... the faster we achieve sustainability, the better.[468]

I don't have any fundamental dislike of hydrocarbons. I simply look at the future and say, "What is the thing that will actually work?" Using a nonrenewable resource obviously will not work.[469]

There are time extensions on the game, but the game is going to end eventually. That should be obvious. If we rely on non-renewables, it's like we're stuck in a room where the oxygen is gradually depleting. We want to get out of that room. The sooner we get out of that room, the better.[470]

Q: How do you respond to people who don't see the problem with extraction?

It is dangerous to be extracting vast quantities of hydrocarbons from deep within the earth and putting them in the atmosphere. Sooner or later, something bad will happen. There are a lot of people, particularly in the US, who are vehemently against electric cars and sustainable energy. It's quite difficult to reason with them.

They'll say, "Well, some scientists don't think climate change is a problem."[471]

> You can find some small number of people that will disagree with anything.

This reminds me of the tobacco industry. For the longest time you'd see ads where they claimed tobacco was healthy for you. It's hard to believe these days, but it's true.

There were reports where there seemed to be a correlation between lung cancer and smoking, but tobacco companies would say, "Our scientists have conducted experiments and they show no relation at all!" It's complete nonsense.[472]

Almost any reasonable scientist would say, "Yes, of course smoking causes lung cancer and all sorts of other bad things. Not definitively but it's extremely likely." Yet the tobacco industry would still say, "Scientists disagree!" because 1 or 2 percent of the scientific community didn't feel that way.

The public just hears "Scientists disagree!" rather than "99 percent of scientists think the other 1 percent are stupid."[473]

The question isn't, "Can you prove we're making the planet warmer?" but, "Can you prove we're not?" And you can't.[474]

It makes me mad when smart, ethical scientists are accused of publishing climate papers for "grant money." They earn peanuts compared to their other opportunities and give that up to help the world. But their accusers earn billions by slowing down the growth of clean energy. Who is more credible?[475]

People often believe things inversely proportional to the evidence. It's so strange.

Given a set of possible explanations, why pick the extremely unlikely one?[476]

Q: So it's not too late to turn things around?

Humanity will solve sustainable energy if we continue to push hard. The future is bright for cheap, abundant energy. It will be possible to use that energy to pull carbon out of the atmosphere. It takes a lot of energy to do that carbon capture, because putting it into the atmosphere releases energy. To pull it out, you need to use a lot of energy.

But if we've got a lot of sustainable energy from wind and solar, we can sequester carbon. We can reverse the CO2 parts per million of the atmosphere and oceans and restore the climate.[477]

> I donated $100 million to a prize for the best carbon capture technology.

We can create as much fresh water as we want. Earth is mostly water. We should call Earth "Water." It's 70 percent water by surface area. We just happen to be on the small bit that's land. With energy, we can turn ocean water into fresh water or irrigation water at low cost.[478]

When you burn fossil fuels, there's all these side reactions and toxic gasses of various kinds. A lot of little particulates that are bad for your lungs. All sorts of bad things are happening, which will go away with sustainable energy. The sky will be cleaner and quieter. The future is going to be good.[479]

The purpose of Tesla was, and remains, accelerating the use of sustainable energy, so we can imagine far into the future and life is still good. That's what "sustainable" means. It's not some silly hippie thing—it matters for everyone.[480]

GOING ALL IN, AGAIN (PAYPAL EARNINGS INTO TESLA)

> When you have a big technology change, it tends to come from new companies.[481]

A lot of entrepreneurial talent and financing goes to the internet. Other sectors like automotive, solar, and space don't see new entrants. Not a lot of entrepreneurs go into those areas, and not a lot of capital goes into those startups.[482]

This is a problem because innovation tends to come from new entrants to an industry. This is Schumpeter's idea of creative destruction. In an oligopoly, no one is forced to innovate.[483] New entrants drive innovation more than anything, which is why I have devoted my efforts to building new companies in those industries.[484]

These industries require quite a bit of capital to get going. My proceeds from PayPal after tax were about $180 million. I thought I would allocate half to SpaceX, Tesla, and SolarCity. I thought that should be fine. I'd have $90 million left, and that's…a lot, you know?[485]

But things cost more and took longer than I thought.[486] Each one ended up costing double what I expected. I thought SpaceX would need $50 million. Tesla, I thought, would need $25 million, maybe $30 million. SolarCity…actually went really well.[487]

I ended up putting $10 million into Solar City, $70 million into Tesla, and $100 million into SpaceX. I literally had to borrow money for rent. It was a close call.[488]

BUILDING THE FIRST PROTOTYPE

I first realized all vehicles would be electric in the early nineties, way before Tesla started. I was studying physics in my sophomore year in college; it was obvious to me even then.[489]

Getting the timing right was important. Lithium-ion batteries were the critical breakthrough needed for compelling electric cars. I knew it became possible to start Tesla because we went from the energy density of lead acid batteries to lithium-ion batteries—about a 4x energy density improvement. If you had a sixty-mile range with a lead-acid battery, you would have about one-hundred-forty-mile range with lithium-ion for the same weight.

A company called AC Propulsion had built a prototype, which had similar specs to what we eventually brought to market as the first Tesla Roadster. It was cool to see it in action, working. I tried hard to convince those guys to commercialize their car but they just did not want to do it.

The car they wanted to make was like an electric Scion. I told them, "You guys, nobody's gonna pay $70,000 for an electric Scion. This is not gonna work. You will sell like fourteen of these things."

Though I also said, "Even though I think this is the dumbest idea ever, I will fund one tenth of it if you can find nine other people."[490]

I thought it would fail, but at least it was something. They didn't actually get it off the ground. Eventually I said, "If you guys are not going to commercialize this, do you mind if I do?"[491]

> We made so many mistakes in the beginning of Tesla. Almost every decision we made was wrong.[492]

The founding principles of Tesla were basically completely wrong. The premise was, "It's not gonna be that hard! We'll take the Lotus Elise, a nice lightweight car, and we'll take AC Propulsion's drive unit technology, put 'er together, and we'll have an electric car! It'll be great!"

Except the AC Propulsion technology could not be industrialized. It was handcrafted electronics. In hot or cold weather, it would respond differently or not at all. It was impossible to scale this technology. You could only have finicky, individually made, superexpensive prototypes.

I remember in the early days giving a test ride to Larry Page and Sergey Brin, whom I've known for a long time. There was some bug in the system and, damn it, the car would only go ten miles an hour. I was in the passenger seat saying, "Guys, I swear, it goes a lot faster than this."

They were kind enough to put a little investment into the company, despite the world's worst demo.[493]

It was just a flat-out burning dumpster fire of stupidity. One example: The chassis had to be redesigned to fit the battery pack and became 40 percent heavier. This invalidated the crash testing Lotus had done.[494]

We ended up using none of the AC Propulsion technology. Something that looks cool and works as an individual prototype does not necessarily scale. Eventually maybe 7 percent of the parts of the original Tesla Roadster were common with the Lotus Elise. It would have been much smarter to start with a clean-sheet design and not try to modify something else.[495]

I was going to start an electric vehicle (EV) company with JB Straubel based on the AC Propulsion prototype. When I asked AC Propulsion if it was okay to do that, they said, "There are some other people who want to create an EV company; would you like to join forces with them?" I said, "OK." That was a huge mistake. JB and I should have just started the company ourselves. My default inclination is to start things from scratch, even more so after this experience.[496]

> The most important thing is to start somewhere, be prepared to question your assumptions, fix what you did wrong, and adapt to reality.[497]

THE MOST IMPORTANT THING IS TO START SOMEWHERE, BE PREPARED TO QUESTION YOUR ASSUMPTIONS, FIX WHAT YOU DID WRONG, AND ADAPT TO REALITY.

BECOMING TESLA'S CEO

The actual error was me trying to have my cake and eat it too: I just wanted to work on the technology and the product. I thought someone else could be the CEO and run the business, because I just like working on technology, product, and design. I was also doing SpaceX at the time, and our rockets were exploding.

I had always wanted to build an electric car company. I thought this is how I could have my cake and eat it too. That was a huge mistake and fundamentally a moral error. When I joined, there were no employees. There was no intellectual property. There was no prototype, no nothing.[498]

I had provided about 95 percent of the money for Tesla, so I could become CEO anytime I wanted. And in the end, I had to frickin' become CEO of Tesla. I didn't want to be, but it was either that or the company was going to die.[499]

> I never wanted to be a CEO, but I learned you could not truly be the chief technology or product officer unless you were the CEO.[500]

Being CEO of two startups at the same time was not appealing. It shouldn't be appealing, by the way, for anyone thinking it was a good idea. It was a terrible idea.[501]

If you're a CEO of a company, the chore level is high, and if you don't do your chores then the company goes to hell. Frankly,

I hate doing chores—who doesn't? There's a whole bunch of personnel and legal issues: things I don't find enjoyable to work on, but if I don't work on them, the company suffers. The sheer volume of work is insane.[502]

The perception of me as a businessperson is fine, but my time is spent almost entirely with the engineering team. I'm a physics guy, an engineer. I'd prefer to be working on products. I do the business stuff because you have to do the business stuff. If you don't do the business stuff, somebody else could do it for you and then you could be in trouble.[503]

I have a habit of biting off more than I can chew and just sitting there with chipmunk cheeks.[504]

SEQUENCED STRATEGY OF TESLA

Tesla is focused on making electric cars more affordable, which is tough. You need high volume to make cars affordable. When we started, other car companies made a lot more cars, so they got much better economies of scale. As we build more cars in higher volume, we make electric cars available to a wider range of people at lower cost.[505]

The first version of a product has both a new-technology problem and a low-volume problem. You want to make your mistakes at a small scale, work the bugs out of the system, then reach for scale.[506]

With a new product, the first thing engineers try to do is make it work. After you make it work, then you optimize and optimize and optimize.[507]

The master plan was:

1. Build a sports car.
2. Use that money to build an affordable car.
3. Use that money to build an even more affordable car.

(While doing above, also provide zero-emission electric power generation options.)[508]

We had to start off with step one, because it was all I could afford with what I made from PayPal. I thought our chances of success were so low, I didn't want to risk anyone's funds but my own in the beginning.[509]

The list of successful car startups is short. The number of American car companies that haven't gone bankrupt is a grand total of two: Ford and Tesla. Starting a car company is idiotic, and an electric car company is idiocy squared.[510]

> **The idea is to drive to mass market as rapidly as possible, at the pace technology matures.**[511]

As a little startup building a car, there was no way we could afford a giant plant to make hundreds of thousands of cars a year. That's the kind of volume you need to make cheap cars, and that plant would cost a billion dollars we didn't have.

Our first car was a sports car, not because we think the world lacks a sports car, but because it was the right entry point for the market. If you have a new technology, the right place to enter is high unit-cost, low unit-volume.[512]

A low-volume car means a much smaller, simpler factory with most things done by hand. Without economies of scale, anything we built would be expensive whether it was an economy sedan or a sports car. Some people would be prepared to pay a high price for a sports car. No one would pay $100K for an electric Honda Civic, no matter how cool it looked.[513]

When a new cell phone or a new laptop comes out, they tend to be expensive at first, because they're figuring out the issues and it takes time to optimize. Over time, with scale, that new technology becomes cheaper and cheaper.[514]

That is the unique and important thing Tesla accomplished. It is not the design of an electric vehicle, an electric vehicle prototype, or even low-volume production of a car. The hard part is not creating a prototype or going into limited production. There have been hundreds of car startups over the years that got that far.[515]

The difficult thing—which has not been accomplished by an American car company in one hundred years—is reaching volume production without going bankrupt. That is the actual hard thing. The last American car company to reach volume production without going bankrupt was Chrysler. That was in the 1920s.[516]

KEEPING TESLA ALIVE

> Tesla is alive by the skin of its teeth. So is SpaceX. If things had gone a little bit the other way, both companies would be dead.

Man, this was grim. I thought this was going to turn into a tale of warning for hubris.[517]

In 2008, SolarCity made a deal with Morgan Stanley, and Morgan Stanley had to renege on the deal because they themselves were running out of money. For a while it looked like all three companies were going to die. I was also going through a divorce. In addition to all that, I was getting dumped on, massively, in the press. That was definitely a low point.[518]

In the midst of this, I faced one of the most difficult choices of my whole life. Tesla and SpaceX were both on the brink of bankruptcy.

I had maybe $30 million or $40 million left. I had two choices: I could put it all into one company, and the other would definitely die. I could split it between Tesla and SpaceX—but if I split it between the two, they both might die.

When you put your blood, sweat, and tears into creating something, building something important—it's like a child.

Which one will I let starve to death?

I couldn't bring myself to do it.

So, I split the money between the two.[519]

Trying to raise money for a startup electric car company in 2008 while GM was going bankrupt was difficult, to say the least. Eventually a subset of the previous investors came in, which included Antonio Gracias, Steve Jurvetson, and Aaron Price, all whom I hold a debt of gratitude to. They said they would invest as much as I put in, so I put in everything. All the money I had left. Literally everything. I didn't have a house. I was staying in Jeff Skoll's spare bedroom.

> (Note from Eric: At this point, Steve Jurvetson might interject with this context about entrepreneurial heroism.
>
> "Elon wrote a check for the entire remainder of his personal wealth to save the company, covering payroll during Christmas when no one else would. The economy was in a bad situation. Goldman just failed a private offering. It was the middle of the financial crisis.
>
> Tesla did not look appealing, either. There was no DOE loan. There was no Daimler deal. The car had a negative gross margin. Oh, and the largest shareholder was pissed off, going AWOL. It was ugly.")[520]

We closed that round at 6:00 p.m. on Christmas Eve 2008. It was the last hour of the last day possible. We would have bounced payroll two days after Christmas.

Eventually, Daimler executives came to visit. They showed up expecting a PowerPoint. While they were on their way over, we dropped a Roadster motor and battery into a Smart Car and let them drive it. They were shocked when it hit 60 mph in four seconds. Daimler ended up investing $50 million. If Daimler had not invested in Tesla at that time, we would have died.[521]

It's definitely stressful when death is inches from your face, trying to eat your face off—like *right there* and the foam is spattering on you.[522]

For a while all I could think was, "We need to live. How do we live?"[523]

At both SpaceX and Tesla in 2008, if we'd paid our suppliers on time we would have gone bankrupt immediately.[524]

THE EDGE OF SANITY

Q: How do you prioritize with so many things going on at once?

Prioritizing has usually been out of desperation, not selection. It's not, "Oh, let's sit back and leisurely decide how we shall spend these resources." It's, "This isn't working, if we don't make it work, we're gonna go bankrupt, so we better make it work."

We messed up almost every aspect of the Model 3 production line. There were so many mistakes, the entire company had to be devoted to fixing them. We took everyone off every other project—we all started working on the Model 3. We had to make it work or there wouldn't be any more Tesla.[525]

There was no choice. We had to get to high-volume production. It was a chicken-and-egg situation. You can't make the car at an affordable price unless you have high volume. Without high volume, you can't sell at an affordable price. So what do you do?[526]

> You take a giant flying leap at high volume and hope you can grab a cliff ledge with your fingertips.[527]

I felt like Indiana Jones running through the temple. There's a huge boulder chasing you and you need to jump across a giant pit in the ground. If you slow down, the boulder will crush you, and if you don't make the leap, you'll die in the pit. That's prioritizing.[528]

Q: How did you motivate the team to do whatever it takes?

I told them we had to go ultrahardcore. They had to prepare for a level of intensity greater than anything they had experienced before.[529]

I lived in the Fremont and Nevada factories for three years fixing that production line, running around like a maniac through every part of that factory, living with the team. I slept on the floor so the team going through a hard time could see me on the floor and know I was not in some ivory tower. Whatever pain they experienced, I had more.[530]

I worked to the edge of sanity. There wasn't any other way to make it work but three years of hell. From 2017 to 2019, I experienced the longest period of excruciating pain in my life. There wasn't any other way, and we still barely made it. We were on the ragged edge of bankruptcy the entire time. Three years of pain, but it had to be done or Tesla would be dead.[531]

At this point, I think I know more about manufacturing than anyone currently alive on Earth.

I can tell you how every damn part in that car is made. That's what happens when you live in the factory for three years.[532]

A WHOLE NEW KIND OF CAR COMPANY

> Ultimately, what we induce other companies to do will have a greater impact than the cars we make ourselves.[533]

Q: A Tesla is a very different product, but how different is Tesla as a company from a traditional auto company?

A typical car company manages a supply chain, assembles vehicles, and sends them to dealers. They might make the engine, but most of the actual technology development and parts manufacturing is done by suppliers. Most of the vehicle software is done by suppliers too. The amount of "real work" done by car companies like GM or Ford is not as much as you think. They don't do sales or service either; dealerships do.[534]

At Tesla, we do our own sales and service. We don't have dealerships.[535] I have made it a principle within Tesla that we should never attempt to make service a profit center. It does not seem right to me when companies make a profit off customers when their product breaks.[536] The best way to experience service is, of course, to not need service.[537]

> If we charge for something, it is not because we want to make things more expensive; it's because we can't figure out how to make it less expensive.[538]

There's a lot of vertical integration at Tesla. We make the battery pack, the power electronics, and the drivetrain ourselves. We're vertically integrated because the pace we needed to move was much faster than the supply chain could move. To the degree you rely on the legacy supply chain, you inherit the legacy constraints—including their speed, costs, and technology.

We do car insurance now, too. Car insurance is a bigger deal than it may seem. A lot of people are paying 30–40 percent as much as their car lease payment for insurance. The car insurance industry is incredibly inefficient because they've got all these middlemen, from the insurance agent all the way to the final reinsurer. There are a half dozen companies each taking a cut.[539]

Insurance is driven by statistics, so even if you're a good driver at twenty years old, it's extremely expensive. Tesla allows for real-time insurance based on how you actually drive the car. If you drive the car in a safer way, you pay lower insurance. Our insurance is based on how you drive, not how people who fit your demographic have driven historically.[540]

Tesla is as much a software company as a hardware company. The software in a Tesla operates the car, the screen, the charging…all developed by us. Then, Tesla built an autopilot AI team from scratch, the best real-world AI team on Earth. We also built a chip team too, because the hardware we could buy wasn't capable of running our AI software.[541]

Q: How important is the look and design of the cars?

> The value of beauty and inspiration is underrated, no question.[542]

If you want to make something beautiful, you must trigger whatever fundamental aesthetic algorithms there are. Our brains have some intrinsic elements that represent beauty, which trigger the emotion of appreciation of beauty in our mind.

I think these are relatively consistent among people. Not completely. Not everyone likes exactly the same thing, but there's a lot of commonality. It is important to combine aesthetic design with functionality.

What was hard about the Model S and Model X was to combine aesthetics and utility, to balance the two. You can make a car look good by giving it certain proportions—making it low and slim. But if you do that, the utility is significantly affected. The big challenge is trying to figure out how to get five adults plus two kids in a seven-seater with high utility *and* keep it looking good. To make a sports car look good is relatively easy. But to make a sedan or an SUV look good is quite difficult.[543]

Another incredibly important design principle is to have it feel bigger on the inside than it looks on the outside. That's also a hard thing to do.[544]

Most people don't consciously notice the small details, but they do subconsciously. Your mind takes in an overall impression. You know if something is appealing or not, even though you may not be able to point out exactly why. That sense is a summation of many details. Most of us experience this as "that's ugly," or "that's beautiful," or "wow, that's elegant," but can't break down why.[545]

You can train yourself. You can make yourself pay attention to "why." You can learn to bring subconscious awareness into conscious awareness. Look closely and carefully. Look at each object's geometry.[546]

Pay attention to the little details. Train yourself to notice them. Notice the nuances of design, shape, form, function, and the way it looks in different lights. Anyone can do this, although it is a double-edged sword, because then you always notice all the little things. Now when something's off—even a little thing—it drives me bananas.

If you're trying to make a perfect product, attention to detail is essential.[547]

GIVE PEOPLE MORE FOR LESS

> Revolutionizing industries is not for the faint of heart.[548]

Q: How do you think about iterating through products to reach a mass market?

The nature of new technology adoption tends to follow an S-curve. People underpredict it in the beginning, because they tend to extrapolate trends in a straight line. Then they'll overpredict it at the midpoint during massive growth. It will take longer than people think at the midpoint, but much shorter than people think at the beginning.[549]

One way to look at technology is like rendering an image in successive levels of detail. The first layer of the image is very blurry and things are out of place. Then with the next pass, it gets a bit more defined and things start to shift into place. And you do another pass and another pass, and eventually it's refined and actually works.[550] It generally takes three major iterations of any major new technology to have it work really, really well.[551]

Progress comes from design and technology improvements as well as scale. Look at the earliest cell phones. In the original *Wall Street* movie in 1987, the guy's walking down the beach with a giant phone, carrying a briefcase to power it. It had like thirty minutes of battery life. Without technology improvements, no amount of money or scale could have made that phone affordable. It took a lot of engineering and design iterations.[552]

In the early days of cell phones, laptops, and gasoline cars, they were considered toys for rich people. You need to go through this phase of having an expensive car available to few in order to build the low-cost car available to many. The first version is simply about making the new technology work. Then, you work to optimize.[553]

We're probably on the thirtieth version of a cell phone, and with each successive design iteration we add more capability. We integrate more parts and figure out better ways to produce it so it gets both better and cheaper. Progress in any new technology takes multiple versions and a large production volume to make it affordable.[554]

Air travel used to be accessible to only a few people. It was insanely expensive and dangerous. Now it is common to fly. The first TVs were rare and expensive. Then big, flat-screen plasma TVs used to be extremely expensive. Now, you can buy an amazing flat-screen plasma for two hundred bucks. It's amazing.[555]

This is also true for electric cars. The strategy for Tesla was to enter at the high end of the market with the Roadster, where customers are prepared to pay a premium. Then move as fast as possible to higher volume and lower prices with each successive model.[556]

The Model S was a sporty four-door family car at roughly half the price point of the Roadster. Then the Model 3 was even more affordable. All free cash flow was plowed back into R&D

to drive down costs and bring the next products to market as fast as possible. When someone bought the Tesla Roadster, they were helping pay for development of the low-cost family car.[557]

Q: Any other unique aspects about Tesla's product philosophy?

Focus on signal over noise. A lot of companies get confused. They spend a lot of money on things that don't actually make the product better. At Tesla, we put all the money into research and development, manufacturing, and design to try and make the cars as good as possible. For any company, ask, "Are the efforts we're expending resulting in a better product or service?" If they're not, stop those efforts.[558]

Also, go for extreme levels of precision. One of the examples we use at Tesla is LEGO blocks. LEGO is super precise. The press-fit comes down to a quarter millimeter or less, and each one is exactly the same. LEGO doesn't work if the press-fit is too soft or too hard. If it's too soft, the press-and-click won't stick; if it's too hard, you can't get it on. They can make something that is a tiny fraction of a millimeter accurate and it's a low-cost plastic toy. If LEGO can be that precise, so can a car.[559]

THE BATTLE OF PUBLIC PERCEPTION

> It should puzzle you that a Tesla crash resulting in a broken ankle is front-page news, yet the many thousands of people who die in US auto accidents each year get almost no coverage.[560]

Q: How do you stay positive when faced with public attacks and misrepresentation, without becoming resentful or cynical?[561]

It does get me down at times. It makes me sad. But at some point you realize these attacks are by people who don't know you and their goal is to generate clicks. If you can detach yourself emotionally (which is not easy) and say, "This person does not know me. They're just writing to get clicks" then it doesn't hurt as much.[562]

It also helps to stay focused on our mission. Tesla's motivation remains to make electric transport as affordable as possible. That informs all our actions.[563]

We put all our money and effort into trying to make the product as compelling as possible. The way to sell any product is through word of mouth. The key is to have a product people love. People will talk about the things they love.[564]

That generates real word of mouth, and that's how our sales have grown. We're not spending money on advertising, public relations, or endorsements. Anyone who buys our car bought it because they like the car, not their impression of the car.⁵⁶⁵

> Tesla does not advertise or pay for endorsements. Instead, we use that money to make the product great.⁵⁶⁶

There are over a million internal combustion engine car fires per year resulting in thousands of deaths, but one Tesla car fire with no injuries gets the biggest headlines. Why the double standard?⁵⁶⁷

The problem is journalists are under constant pressure to get maximum clicks. They either earn advertising dollars or get fired. It's a tricky situation, since Tesla doesn't advertise and fossil fuel companies and legacy car companies are among the world's biggest advertisers.⁵⁶⁸

Regulators tend to pay a disproportionate amount of attention to whatever is in the press. This is an objective fact. And Tesla generates a lot of press. In the United States, there are about forty thousand automotive deaths per year. But if there are four in a Tesla, they'll probably receive a thousand times more press than any other incident.⁵⁶⁹

The reality is a Tesla, like most electric cars, is over 500 percent *less* likely to catch fire than gas combustion engine cars, which carry massive amounts of highly flammable fuel. Why is this never mentioned?⁵⁷⁰

FOUNDING SOLARCITY

Q: How did SolarCity fit into the vision for Tesla?

The earth is almost entirely solar powered today. The only reason we're not a frozen ice ball at three degrees Kelvin is the sun. The sun is responsible for precipitation. It's responsible for the vast majority of the ecosystem. We could say the entire earth is solar powered. That may not be super obvious to people. Also, the energy we consume to power civilization today is actually a tiny amount of the total energy the sun sends in our direction.[571]

I wouldn't say there was a particular epiphany to start SolarCity. I was at Burning Man with my cousins. They were thinking about what company to start after their first startup, called Everdream, sold to Dell. They built software that enabled companies to manage tens of thousands of computers.[572]

I was trying to convince them to do solar, because I thought it was an area that needed really good entrepreneurs. I was already somewhat overcommitted at the time. I said, "If you guys do a solar company, I'll fund you and give whatever guidance I can provide."[573]

I thought it was really important for great entrepreneurs to build in solar because it wasn't doing well as an industry. People were not focusing on the right problem. The industry acted like the solar panel production was the main problem. It's *a* problem, but it's not the most important problem. The panel is somewhat commoditized at this point. Making standard-efficiency solar panels is about as hard as making drywall. It's easy. In fact, making drywall is probably harder.[574]

The thorny problem is figuring out how to get solar on tens of thousands, eventually hundreds of thousands, of rooftops. You've got to reroof millions of buildings, figure out how the grid interconnects work, and then manage all those systems.

With hundreds of thousands of distributed systems, managing them all is tough. It is a really complex distributed energy company. This played to their strengths: creating scalable software for managing computers in a distributed fashion.

The SolarCity team did an awesome job. I would show up to the board meetings asking, "What's the good news this time?" They did an amazing job with almost no help from me.[575]

We want to create a well-integrated beautiful solar-roof-with-battery product. This empowers individuals to be their own utility, then scale that throughout the world. One ordering experience, one installation, one service contact, one phone app.

We can't do this well if Tesla and SolarCity are different companies. We needed to break down the barriers of being separate companies. That they were separate at all is largely an accident of history. They have similar origins and pursue the same overarching goal of sustainable energy. When Tesla was ready to scale Powerwall (our home battery for energy storage) and SolarCity was ready to provide a differentiated solar system for energy generation, the time had come to bring them together.[576]

BUILDING SPACEX

Building mass-market electric cars was inevitable.

It would have happened without me.

But becoming a space-faring civilization is not inevitable.[577]

THE ONLY ONE CRAZY ENOUGH FOR SPACE

> I've always been optimistic. If I wasn't optimistic, I wouldn't be attempting all these crazy things. I must be pathologically optimistic, I suppose.[578]

The origin of SpaceX was trying to figure out why we had not sent anyone to Mars. The obvious next step after Apollo was to send people to Mars.[579]

Every year I'd look at the NASA website, and there didn't seem to be a date for it. We were able to go to the moon in 1969. Our last mission to the moon was in 1972. Now here we are *half a century* later and we still have not gone back to the moon. It would be extremely tragic if Apollo was the high-water mark for humanity, if the moon was as far as we got.[580]

The space shuttle could only take people to low earth orbit. Then the space shuttle retired, and the United States could take no one to orbit. The trend was dwindling down to nothing. Does this mean we've peaked as a civilization?[581]

If you had asked people in 1969 what the world would look like in fifty years, they would have expected a base on the moon and some people visiting Mars. Maybe even a base on Mars. They would expect orbiting space hotels and other awesome stuff.[582]

If you told them, "Well, we have a device smaller than a deck of cards with access to all the world's information, and you can talk to anyone instantly on planet Earth. But the United States will not be able to send anyone to orbit," they would have called bullshit. "You have all of that, and nothing is happening in space?!" After we sold PayPal in 2001, I was trying to figure out why.[583]

The original idea for SpaceX wasn't to create a company. It was to figure out why we hadn't sent people to Mars. I thought maybe we'd lost the will to explore. I thought we had to *create* the will to explore. But that was wrong.

We have not lost the will to explore; people just did not think there was a way forward. If people don't think there's a way, then they won't continuously bash their head against the wall for progress.[584]

> There must be things to inspire us—that make you proud to be a member of humanity.[585]

The Apollo moon landing was an example of that. Only a handful of people went to the moon—and yet actually we all went to the moon. We went with them vicariously. We shared in that adventure. No one would say that was a bad idea—that Apollo wasn't great. We need more of those.[586]

> The United States is a distillation of the human spirit of exploration. It's fundamental to the psyche.
>
> Once people realized, "There is a way to do this," we got a lot of support.[587]

I EXPECTED TO LOSE EVERYTHING

When something is important enough, you do it even if the odds are not in your favor.[588]

When I started them, I guessed both SpaceX and Tesla each had a probability of less than 10 percent to succeed.

I don't look at ideas and ask, "What is the rank-ordered list of best business opportunities from a financial standpoint?" I look for problems that are important to fix for people now *and* for the future to be good.

If one were to do a risk-adjusted rate of return estimate on opportunities, building rockets and building cars would be pretty close to the bottom of the list. They would be the dumbest things you could possibly do.

Company stock value is not a metric by which I judge my own achievements.[589]

I had a lot of friends try to talk me out of starting a rocket company, because they thought it was crazy. Everyone thought it was a crazy idea. Some people had actually tried to start rocket companies before and failed. They tried to talk me out of it too.[590]

One good friend compiled a bunch of footage of rocket failures and forced me to watch it. I said, "I've seen them all already."[591]

I think these people misunderstood my premise. When I started SpaceX, it was not with the expectation of success. I thought the most likely outcome was failure.

Their premise for talking me out of it was, "You're going to lose the money you invest." I replied, "Well, that was my expectation anyway, so I don't really mind!"

I mean, I mind losing money, but it's not like I was trying to figure out the rank-ordered best way to invest my money and on that basis chose space. I didn't think, "I could do real estate, or invest in shoemaking, and—whoa! Space has the highest ROI!" That was not my premise.[592]

There have been many times where I expected to lose everything. Who starts a car company and a rocket company expecting them to succeed? Certainly not me. I thought they both had a low chance of success, less than 10 percent. Maybe 1 percent, I don't know. Frankly, I wasn't wrong.[593]

We must be optimistic. There's no point in being pessimistic. It just doesn't help. My theory is you'd rather be optimistic and wrong about the future than pessimistic and right. If you're pessimistic, you're going to be miserable. Might as well enjoy the journey.[594]

Q: How did you go about creating belief and support for the Mars mission?

> If you're trying to convince the public to do something, you have to think about what will excite people.

What message are we going to try to convey? What will people respond to? What would I respond to if I was an objective member of the public?

I thought we could send a small greenhouse to the surface of Mars, with seeds and a nutrient gel to hydrate the seeds upon landing.[595]

The greenhouse mission would be the first life on another planet, as far as we knew. The farthest life had ever traveled. We would have a great picture of green plants on a red background. That's the money shot. People tend to respond to precedents and superlatives.

I thought getting a greenhouse on Mars would get people excited about sending humans there. My original goal was to get the public excited, to get NASA's budget increased to get a mission to Mars funded.[596]

I was willing to spend half the money I got from PayPal, so $90 million, on this mission with no expectation of return. This was just something important to accomplish. If I spent $90 million to get NASA a bigger budget, which resulted in us going to Mars, that would be a good outcome.[597]

Also, I was trying to figure out if I could afford to build a spacecraft. I wanted to budget for two missions because if we only did one and it failed, it might actually deter people from trying in the future.[598]

I was able to get the cost of the spacecraft, communications, and the little greenhouse down. But the one thing I couldn't compress was the cost to launch. There were only a few options, and the US options were way too expensive. I ended up going to Russia three times to try to buy the biggest intercontinental ballistic missile (ICBM) in the Russian nuclear fleet. That didn't work out.[599]

In doing this, I realized what we really need to do is improve the technology of space transportation.[600] I wanted to hold out hope that humans could be a space-faring civilization, out there among the stars. There was no chance of that unless a new company was started to create revolutionary rockets.[601]

If a startup didn't do something to advance rocket technology, it wouldn't happen. Either it's coming from a startup or it's not happening at all. A small chance of success is better than no chance of success. So I started SpaceX in mid-2002, expecting to fail.[602]

Q: Why did you decide to fund SpaceX yourself?

After PayPal was sold, I started debating between working on solar, electric cars, or space. I figured space would be the least likely to succeed, so least likely to attract other entrepreneurs.

Nobody else was crazy enough to do space. I thought I'd better work on space first.

My first idea, the greenhouse mission, would have a 100 percent chance of losing all the money associated with it. If anything, starting a rocket company had less than a 100 percent chance of losing all the money associated with it. From my perspective, it was actually less risky than the first idea, which was just paying to send the greenhouse to Mars.[603]

> The likeliest outcome is I will lose all my money.
>
> But what's the alternative? No progress in space exploration?
>
> We've got to give this a shot, or we're stuck on Earth forever.[604]

I would not recommend a space company to first-time entrepreneurs. Space is advanced entrepreneuring. You're better off starting something that requires little capital first. Space is definitely a high-capital effort.[605]

I'm a big believer in this: Don't ask investors to invest their money if you're not prepared to invest your money. It doesn't seem right to me to ask other people to invest if you don't also invest. I'd rather lose my money than any of my friends' money or investors' money.[606]

I didn't even seek investor funding for the first three rounds of SpaceX because the first thing investors want to ask you is, "Tell us about prior successes in this field. What can we compare this to?" When you have about zero in the success category and a cemetery full of failures, they're not too keen. Rockets are pretty far out of the comfort zone of most venture capitalists.

We were able to get venture funding after we demonstrated we were almost able to get to orbit. Credit goes to Founders Fund, my compatriots from PayPal: Peter Thiel, Luke Nosek, Ken Howery, and the guys. They invested before we got to orbit, so credit to them.

Rockets are hard. I had never made physical stuff before SpaceX, let alone rockets. I had to show I could actually make stuff.[607]

Once we started building a space launch company, I predicated the strategic plan on a known market, something I know for a fact exists: the need to put small- to medium-sized satellites into orbit. We served that need initially. With that as a base of revenue, we could eventually move into the human transportation market.[608]

First, we built an orbital launch vehicle. A high mass-efficiency launch vehicle targeted to solving the satellite delivery market. Our approach was to make this a solid, sound business from the beginning.[609]

The long-term aims of the company were always human transportation. But I think the smart strategy was to first go for cargo delivery, putting satellites into orbit. Our eventual upgrade path was to build Starship, the successor to Saturn V rocket, a superheavy-lift vehicle that could be used for setting up a moon base or doing a Mars mission. That is our holy grail objective.[610]

ROCKETS FROM FIRST PRINCIPLES

> I was trying to figure out if there was something fundamentally superexpensive about rockets.[611]

Q: How did you determine whether your vision for SpaceX had the potential to succeed?

How could the Russians build low-cost rockets? It's not like we drive Russian cars, fly Russian planes, or have Russian kitchen appliances. The US is a pretty competitive place, and we should be able to build a cost-efficient launch vehicle.[612]

I started reading quite a bit about rockets, trying to understand why they're so friggin' expensive. It used to be $60 million to build the Delta II. Now, a Delta II costs $100 million to make. Crazy number. Delta II is a relatively small rocket! The bigger rockets are anywhere from $200 to $400 million.

> I was pretty mad, and when I get mad I try to reframe the problem.[613]

I looked at the suppliers NASA had been relying on. With suppliers like Boeing and Lockheed, you're screwed.[614]

One problem with those big aerospace firms is incredible

aversion to risk. Even if better technology is available, they still use legacy components, often ones that were developed in the 1960s. Everyone is trying to optimize their ass-covering.[615]

Second, there's a tendency in big aerospace companies to outsource everything. That's been trendy in many industries, but aerospace has done it to a ridiculous degree. They outsource to subcontractors, and then the subcontractors outsource to sub-subcontractors, and so on. You have to go four or five layers down to find somebody actually doing real work—cutting metal, shaping atoms. Every level above that tacks on cost—it's overhead to the fifth power. I began to understand why things were so expensive.[616]

Boeing and Lockheed just want their cost-plus gravy trains. When you've had success for too long, you lose the desire to take risks. We can't get to Mars with that system. They have an incentive to never finish the job.[617]

There wasn't really a good reason for rockets to be so expensive. Rockets could be a lot cheaper *even if they were still expendable*. But, *if* one could make them reusable, like airplanes, then the cost of rocketry and space travel would both drop dramatically.[618]

I put together a feasibility study with a team of engineers who were involved in all major launch vehicle developments over the last thirty years. We met over a number of Saturdays in early 2001 to find the smartest way to approach launch cost and reliability, and we came up with a default design.[619]

It was fortunate timing. The feasibility study finished around the time we agreed to sell PayPal to eBay. So coincidently with that sale, I moved down to Los Angeles, the biggest concentration of aerospace talent in the world.[620]

Q: Did people give you a hard time for this? It seems like a lot of people were saying "Elon is a software guy. Why is he working on hardware?"

One hundred percent. A lot of the press from that time is still online. They kept calling me an "internet guy" attempting to build a rocket company. We got ridiculed quite a bit.

It does sound absurd. "Internet guy starts rocket company" doesn't sound like a recipe for success, frankly, so I don't hold it against them. It does sound improbable, and I agreed. It was improbable.[621]

I didn't study rocket science but have picked it up along the way.[622]

I didn't really know how to start a rocket company. The first three launches failed. I did not hit the bull's-eye.[623]

KEEPING SPACEX ALIVE

> SpaceX is in this for the long haul and, come hell or high water, we are going to make this work.[624]

I thought if we couldn't get to orbit within three failures, we deserved to die. That was my going-in proposition.[625]

In 2006, our first rocket landed a couple hundred yards away from the launch site in tiny fragments. The second attempt failed too. But, we got further each time.[626] In 2008, we had the third failure in a row of the Falcon rocket. I had only budgeted for three attempts.[627]

That's when I split all the money I had left between Tesla and SpaceX. It was enough to afford a fourth launch at SpaceX, if we moved super fast.[628]

I collected everyone in the conference room and said, "We have one last rocket. Get your shit together, go back to the island, and launch it. You have six weeks."[629]

Here was my email to the team: "There should be absolutely zero question that SpaceX will prevail in reaching orbit and demonstrating reliable space transport. For my part, I will never give up and I mean never. Thank you for your hard work. Now, on to flight four."[630]

If we didn't succeed, we would be pointed to as a reason people shouldn't even try these things. We must do whatever is necessary to keep going.[631]

> I don't ever give up. I'd have to be dead or completely incapacitated.[632]

It was an interesting exercise in karma. After I got ousted by the PayPal coup leaders, I could have said "You guys suck," but I didn't. If I'd done that, Founders Fund wouldn't have come through with an investment in SpaceX in 2008 and the company would be dead. Karma may be real.[633]

If the fourth launch hadn't worked, that would have been curtains. I had no money left. It was a pretty close thing. We would have joined the graveyard of prior rocket startups.[634]

I thought the odds of the fourth launch working were better than 50 percent. There was just a little change in the thrust transient of the first-stage engine we couldn't see on the ground. That made the difference. Fortunately, the fourth SpaceX launch worked.[635]

> We almost went down as the company that made it to orbit, then died.

When it worked, my cortisol levels were clinically high. I couldn't feel celebratory. There was no jubilation. I was too stressed. Getting to orbit meant, "Okay, we're not going to die today." We'll live a little bit longer. I just felt relief.[636]

But it was short-lived. We were still in a tough position. It was not like we had customers lined up. Even the fourth launch working wasn't enough to succeed. We also needed a big contract to keep us alive.[637]

LANDING NASA CONTRACTS

After the successful launch, as I was scrambling to fundraise for Tesla in 2008, NASA called out of the blue to tell me SpaceX had won a contract. I couldn't believe it. I screamed, "I LOVE NASA. YOU GUYS ROCK," then hung up. I called our president, Gwynne Shotwell, and told her to immediately sign whatever deal NASA offered.[638]

It felt like I had been blindfolded and taken out to the firing squad. Then they yelled, "Fire" and the guns just went "click." No bullets. Then they let me free. Sure, I was glad to be alive. But I was still pretty fucking nervous.[639]

My estimate of success was not far off.

We just made it by the skin of our teeth.

We had developed the Dragon spacecraft somewhat opportunistically. NASA announced they were going to retire the space shuttle, and they didn't have the budget to develop a new vehicle with cargo transport capability to the space station.

They put it out to bid for the first time in NASA history. It was quite a big step, and we were lucky enough to win one of those contracts. Then, the other company wasn't able to execute, and SpaceX ended up being the primary means of transporting cargo to and from the space station.[640]

Our rocket ended up costing around $6 million, super low compared to other rockets in that class, which were about $25 million. We're about a quarter of the price of Boeing or Lockheed. Once it was reusable, payload delivery could be two orders of magnitude cheaper.[641]

After we did the first two space station resupply missions, which thankfully both worked, NASA said, "What about astronaut transport?" They put out a big competition and awarded two contracts for astronaut transport, one to Boeing and one to SpaceX. Now, we transport astronauts to and from the space station.[642]

YOU HAVE TO BLOW THINGS UP

> The first goal is to make the damn thing work—
> we'll optimize it later.

We want to push the envelope. If you don't push the envelope, you cannot achieve the goal of a fully and rapidly reusable rocket with high payload. It's not possible. You have to go close to the edge on margins.[643]

We intentionally iterate the design of the Starship at SpaceX rapidly. This is a fundamentally different optimization for Starship versus a polar extreme like our Dragon capsule. Since Dragon now carries crew, there can be no failures, ever. Everything's going to be tested. There can never be a failure, ever, for any reason whatsoever. With human crew in a developed vehicle, we're in extreme conservatism mode.

Falcon is a little less conservative. It is possible for us to have, say, a failure with a booster on landing. That's not the end of the world. Early Starship models were the polar opposite of Dragon. We were iterating rapidly to learn.[644]

Q: Is that different from other space programs?

NASA's space shuttle had almost no iteration because there were people on board. You can't be blowing up shuttles. That lack of iteration was a problem. There were a lot of issues they were aware of, but people were too afraid to make changes to a design that had already worked. There was risk-reward asymmetry. If you make a change and something goes wrong, big punishment. If you make a change and it goes right, small reward.

They had seen the issues with the O-ring and the insulation coming off and hitting the wing before, but there had not been a catastrophe. They figured it was good enough because it worked before. But that's like Russian roulette: "Look, I've pulled the trigger and I'm fine."

It's hard to iterate when people are on board every mission. Starship does not have anyone on board during early trials so we can blow things up, learn, and iterate. That's really helpful. To improve safety, you need to fly a lot and have a lot of redundancy. So if you lose an engine on the booster, it doesn't matter. Even losing multiple engines shouldn't matter.[645]

We don't want to design to eliminate every risk. Otherwise, we will never get anywhere.[646]

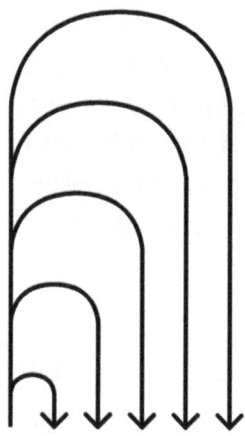

WE DON'T WANT TO DESIGN TO ELIMINATE EVERY RISK.
OTHERWISE, WE WILL NEVER GET ANYWHERE.

Before every Starship launch, we go through the list of risks we predict, which we call the "risk list." If you look at various reasons why we blew up, none of the reasons they blew up were on our "risk list." There's a crazy amount of new technology, all evolving simultaneously. We need time and trials to iron out the unknown unknowns.[647]

Q: What is the big-picture vision SpaceX is iterating toward?

The overarching optimization is: "What is the fastest time to a city on Mars?"

Then subset → fastest time to a fully usable rocket.

And subset → fastest time to orbit.[648]

Initial production was simply a learning exercise. None of the initial designs will be long term. We're just trying to learn in the shortest period of time. The early Starship assembly yard looked like a garage shop, to be frank. It's weird—we have superadvanced technology being built in a tent in a parking lot.

Early versions of Starship didn't even have doors. We didn't need doors. We did need to be superfocused on getting to orbit. Then superfocused on getting the ship back. Doors were just unnecessary complexity. The first ten ships (or more) we won't get back from orbit. We probably won't be flying them again. Maybe once or twice—if we're lucky.[649]

> Eliminate what isn't necessary to solve the key problem.[650]

BUILDING THE JUST BARELY POSSIBLE

> I was told many times rocket reusability was impossible.[651]

One of the hardest engineering problems known to man is making a reusable orbital rocket.

We have reusability in bicycles, cars, and airplanes. It's bizarre to not have reusability in another form of transport. It would be insane to chuck a boat away after every trip. Getting one trip every four days would not cut it in a car. But this is how rockets have worked thus far.[652]

The design goal is immediate reflight. Refill propellants and go again, just like any other mode of transport. This is gigantic.[653]

> Getting to orbit was solved in the 1950s. The math clearly demonstrates there is no point in another expendable rocket; you have to achieve reusability.[654]

It's not like other rocket scientists were huge idiots who wanted to throw their rockets away all the time. It's hard to make something like this. Nobody has ever succeeded, and for a good reason. Earth's gravity is heavy. On Mars this would be no problem. Moon, piece of cake. On Earth, fucking hard. Just barely possible.

A fully reusable orbital system would be one of the biggest breakthroughs in the history of humanity. That's why it hurts my brain. We're just a bunch of monkeys. How did we even get this far? It beats me. We were swinging through the trees eating bananas not long ago.[655]

> Can you imagine if human civilization continued at the current pace of technological advancement for another million years? Where would we be?

I told my team, "Imagine there was a pallet of cash plummeting through the atmosphere and it was going to burn up and smash into tiny pieces. Would you try to save it? You probably would."[656]

When people tried to make a reusable system before, they would conclude success was not one of the possible outcomes. In government programs, of course, the program would still continue for quite some time. It's funny but it's true.[657]

The space shuttle attempted some level of reusability, but it ended up costing more per flight than an expendable vehicle of equivalent capability. For a long time, people pointed to the space shuttle as an example of why attempting reusability was dumb. But you can't take a single example and make an entire theory out of it.[658]

I wasn't sure if it was possible when we started SpaceX, but after a few years of work I became convinced. Full and rapid reuse is possible. It is possible to make this work, and that gave me hope. Of course, just because something is possible does not mean it will occur.[659]

> The first step is to establish that something is possible, then the probability it will occur.[660]
>
> In no prior design was full reusability one of the possible outcomes.[661]

SpaceX's Falcon 9 was the first rocket with any reusability. We bring the boosters back and refly them. Only the upper stage is expended. Falcon 9 is not *rapidly* reusable because most boosters land on a ship in the ocean. It takes a while to bring it back, fuel, and reuse it. Falcon 9 first had reusability measured in months, then weeks, and now finally days. But, the efficiency is limited. We can't bring it lower than several days.[662]

Knock on wood, Falcon 9 is the most reliable rocket in the world and launches about every two to three days.[663] Every one has come home safely, which is the most important thing. We learned a tremendous amount from the Falcon program that fed into the Starship program.[664] We wouldn't have been able to make Starship without the benefit of Falcon 9.[665]

> Nobody thought this was possible. But we're not breaking any laws of physics, so we knew it was possible.[666]

Starship is the largest flying object of any kind. It's five thousand tons at liftoff, much heavier than any other aircraft, ever. The body diameter is nine meters (roughly fifty feet). It will get taller with newer versions too. And it's going straight up; aircraft don't go straight up. It's an insanely gigantic thing, twice the size of Saturn V, previously the largest rocket ever built.[667]

There could be other solutions too, but this will work. The first order of business was to get one that works. Now we optimize.[668] Full and rapid reusability will work. It's just a question of how many attempts we need to make it work, and then make it work really well.[669]

It has to be true reuse, which means *rapid* and *complete* reuse. The problem with the space shuttle was only a portion of the system came back, and the reusable parts were incredibly difficult to refurbish. Reuse matters more if it's rapid and complete—if the only thing we do between flights is maintenance and refuel, like an airplane.[670]

If there is no major work required between flights, then the cost of a flight approaches the cost of propellant. Nearly 80 percent of Starship's propellant is liquid oxygen, and a little over 20 percent methane, which are both very low-cost fuels. The fuel cost of a flight is maybe a million dollars or less.[671]

> Full and rapid reusability is the holy grail of rocketry because then you're only constrained by propellant costs.[672]

Q: What made you remove the landing legs?

We fight to save mass constantly, especially with the reusable upper stage, where nobody has ever succeeded.

Again here, we try to think in the limit of physics. The problem with landing legs is they add mass, we have to protect them during reentry, and we have to get a giant rocket from wherever it landed back onto the launch stand. That's tricky. I was trying to think of the limit. What's the fastest way to achieve reusability?

It would be to land on the launch stand. Why not just have it land on the arms of the tower it launches from?[673]

This is the best-case outcome for rapid reuse. It gets caught by the same arms that placed it in the launch ring. In principle, the superheavy booster can be reflown within an hour of landing. It comes back in about five minutes one way and then it gets caught by the tower arms, placed back in the launch mount, and then we refill propellant in about thirty to forty minutes and place a ship on top of it.[674]

When we first talked about it, it sounded batshit crazy. To custom-build a giant tower to catch the heaviest flying object ever made with mechanical arms. Pluck it out of the air. But we did it.[675]

It's an epic sight: giant robot arms catching a giant rocket. This is much more efficient than having landing legs on the rocket itself.[676]

> I call it rapidly reusable, reliable rockets. RRRR. Space pirates.[677]

OPTIMIZING FOR MASS TO MARS

The thing we optimize for at SpaceX is cost per ton to orbit. When the goal is low cost per ton of payload to orbit, you can't cheat.

All early rockets were a test program. We expected them to explode. It's weird if they don't explode, frankly. To get a lot of payload to orbit at low cost, you have to run everything close to the edge.

To get a meaningful payload to orbit, scale is important. We need to make things big. There is value to scale here. You don't see everything shipped by small pickup trucks; you see semi trailers. You see giant ocean cargo ships, not a bunch of small boats with outboard motors. Scale has value in itself. For example, the same computer that controls a tiny rocket controls the big rocket. The percentage weight of the electronics is significant in a small rocket but becomes vanishingly small in a big rocket.[678]

The focus is to minimize cost per ton of payload to orbit, the surface of the moon, or Mars. I'll give you a sense of just how much we need to improve it. Right now, the cost per landed ton to the surface of Mars is more than a billion dollars. You can't count the heat shield, parachute, or landing systems—only the useful stuff. In the case of the Mars rovers, it's really just the rover. That is the useful thing. The rover weighs about a ton and costs a billion dollars to get to Mars. So currently it costs roughly a billion dollars per ton to Mars.[679]

To build a self-sustaining city on Mars, that cost will have to be less than one hundred thousand dollars a ton. That would be ten thousand times better than the current state of the art, to put things into perspective.[680]

That's how much improvement is needed. Not a 10,000 percent increase, a 10,000-times increase. That's what Starship is intended to do: be ten thousand times better than the current state of the art. Orders and orders and orders of magnitude better. But, we're not breaking any laws of physics. This is possible.[681]

> When we started the Starship design it seemed utterly insane. Now it's gone from utterly insane to merely late.[682]

With full reusability, Starship 3 will cost significantly less per flight than tiny Falcon 1. That's the difference between a fully reusable rocket and an expendable rocket. The fully reusable rocket with low-cost propellant actually costs less than a tiny expendable rocket.[683] By analogy, the cost of flying a 747 is obviously much less than a small airplane that gets thrown away.

Falcon 1 gets about half a ton to orbit. The Starship 3 will send four hundred times more payload for less than the cost of a Falcon 1. It's mind-boggling that the giant thing can cost so much less than the small thing.[684]

A lot of people talk a lot about the number of launches to orbit per year, but this is not really what matters. What really matters is the total useful payload to orbit per year. If these were ocean ships, you'd be comparing a dinghy to a supertanker. They're not the same.[685]

> There must be things you're excited about, that you're glad to be alive for.
>
> For me, this is the most important reason to pursue the establishment of life on Mars.[686]

There are various "great filters" that have the potential to end civilizations. One of the "great filters" to pass is whether we become a multiplanet species. Will humanity be one of those species that passes the great filter of going beyond one planet?[687]

To become multiplanetary, the breakthrough we need to create is a rapidly reusable interplanetary transport system. This is right on the edge of impossible.[688]

That's the breakthrough SpaceX is really trying to achieve. What we've done so far is good; it's better. But it has been evolutionary—not yet revolutionary. We need the revolutionary thing to work.[689]

PART IV

ON BEHALF OF HUMANITY

There is something special—far more rewarding than money—about working with an epic team to make breakthroughs.[690]

BUILDING OUR FUTURE

> I can't emphasize this enough: As long as we push hard and are not complacent, the future is going to be great.[691]

COMPANIES ARE PHILANTHROPY

> If you care about the reality of goodness instead of the perception of it, philanthropy is extremely difficult.
>
> If philanthropy is acting from a love of humanity—my companies are philanthropy.[692]

Q: What do you say to people who criticize you for not "having your name on a hospital wing" or making other nonprofit donations?

I do have a small foundation. I am giving some money away. But generally, if there's a way to fix something within the market system, building a company is the better way to do it. Sometimes there isn't or there are complications to it.[693]

If it's possible to solve a problem with a profitable venture then that's the best thing to do. In the grand scheme of things, there are a few failures in the market that have to be addressed with a nonprofit. There are some, but not many.[694]

SpaceX, Tesla, Neuralink, and the Boring Company are philanthropy. SpaceX is trying to ensure the long-term survival of humanity as a multiple-planet species. We also provide global internet through Starlink. That is love of humanity. Tesla is accelerating sustainable energy. This is a love-based mission. Neuralink is trying to help solve brain injuries and the existential risk of AI. That is love of humanity. The Boring Company is trying to save people's time by solving traffic, which is hell for most people. That is also love of humanity.[695]

My fundamental intent is to improve the probability of the future being good. SpaceX and Tesla will do more good for humanity than anything I could do with philanthropy. It is difficult to give away money effectively if you care about the money actually doing good, not merely having the perception of doing good.[696]

Tesla sells twice as many electric vehicles as the rest of electric car makers in the United States combined. Tesla has done more to help the environment than all other companies combined. Therefore, it would be fair to say as a leader of that company I've done more for the environment than any other single human on Earth. I care about the reality of goodness, not the perception of it.

What I see all over the place is people who care about looking good while doing evil. Fuck them.[697]

I care about reality. Perception be damned.[698]

COMPANIES CREATE WEALTH FOR ALL

I don't disrupt something for the sake of disrupting it. My focus is making a product that improves quality of life for people.[699]

If the output is more valuable than the inputs, that creates a profit. Profit shows you have a useful company. But in a high-growth scenario, you need a lot more inputs for *future* output, so for a while you have negative cash flow and lack of profitability, which we had early on at Tesla. In the long term, of course, that has to be fixed. There can't be a negative cash flow in the long term.[700]

If you create a company that produces products and services better than what existed before, wealth is created. If you have some ownership in that company, wealth accrues to you. Doing good work gives you the right to allocate more capital.[701]

Sometimes people equate wealth with consumption, but they're obviously not the same thing. Consumption is fun, but capital allocation is a job.

> If people want to get upset about something, excess consumption is more reasonable than being upset about someone having a high net worth.[702]

Warren Buffett has a high net worth because he's doing a useful job allocating capital for the economy. He's very skilled at it, and he should probably keep doing it. But he is not engaged in insane, conspicuous consumption.[703]

Warren Buffett sits there and reads all these super boring annual reports. Does anybody want that job? He is constantly reading tedious annual reports of companies, including the minutiae of accounting and deciding whether to allocate capital into Coke or Pepsi. I don't want that job.[704]

I'm not claiming I have no money. But when people hear a big number for my net worth, they think I have that much cash, and I'm sitting on the cash doing nothing, hoarding resources. No, that value *is* the stock of these companies. Net worth just calculates my ownership of these companies, if you add them up. It's not as though I've got billions of dollars sitting in a bank account.[705]

> **Just as my money was the first into Tesla, it will be the last out.[706]**

The alternative to keeping the stock would be to say, "Okay, let's give the stock to the government or someone else." Then the government would control the companies and be running things.[707]

A lot of the push for higher government involvement or expropriation of assets to the government is from politicians. What they are saying is those resources shouldn't be in control of individuals who built them, but instead should be under government control. They're basically saying they want control of the assets.[708]

I think the profit motive is good if the rules of an industry are properly set up. There's nothing wrong with profit. Profit just means people are paying you more for whatever you're creating than you're spending to create it. That's a good thing. If that's not the case, you'll soon be out of business, and rightfully so, because you're not adding enough value.[709]

A few people do bad things to achieve profit, but that's quite unusual, because the rules are mostly set up correctly. Not perfect, but mostly correct.[710]

It is insanely hard to build and ship useful products to a large number of people. There's a hell of a difference between a company that has shipped a product and one that hasn't. It's night and day. Once you ship products, is the value of the output worth more than the cost of the inputs? Again insanely difficult, especially with hardware.[711]

> If you create great products and services that create wealth, that should be applauded.
>
> You increased the standard of living of the country and perhaps of the world.

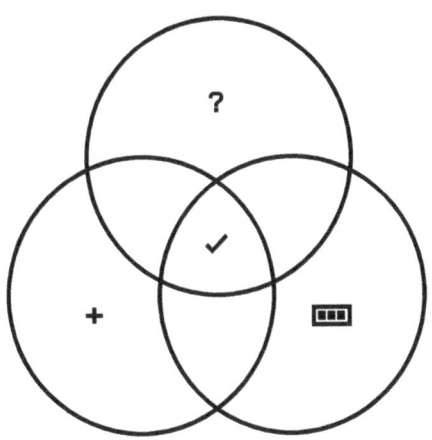

WORK ON THINGS THAT YOU FIND INTERESTING, FULFILLING, AND THAT CONTRIBUTE SOME GOOD TO THE REST OF SOCIETY.

COMPANIES TO START

> Work on things that you find interesting, fulfilling, and that contribute some good to the rest of society.[712]

Q: What are some areas you see where people could build important new technology?

For five years people asked me where I saw opportunities and I'd say "tunneling." But nobody did anything. It was initially a joke, but we created the Boring Company and did a test tunnel in LA. People still didn't believe us. Then we did our first operational tunnel in Vegas.[713]

There are still tremendous opportunities in tunneling. The world needs tunnels. All major cities have traffic, and tunnels can massively improve people's quality of life by making it easy to travel from one place to another. They can be further expanded to long-distance travel. If you draw a vacuum on the tunnel, you can go extremely fast. Faster than a plane or high-speed rail. I'd still recommend someone—please—start a tunneling company.[714]

Another company to start would be anything to do with genetics. If you can solve genetic diseases, you can prevent dementia or Alzheimer's with genetic reprogramming. That would be wonderful.[715]

> Synthetic RNA is revolutionary in medicine. Most people are not aware just how much of a revolution this is.
>
> This is like medicine going from analog to digital.[716]

RNA (ribonucleic acid) or MRNA (messenger RNA) are basically synthetic viruses. I think people don't appreciate what's going on—this is the digitization of medicine. You can create an RNA or DNA (deoxyribonucleic acid) sequence like a computer program and encapsulate it in a lipid shell, so it looks like a tasty treat for your cells. This is the future of medicine.[717]

You can do almost anything. You could probably figure out how to turn someone into a literal butterfly. Your cells are tiny biological computers. They execute just like old-school computers, where you feed it a tape or punch card. Your cells do whatever their punch card says. That was a big eye-opener, understanding the potential of RNA.[718]

You could start a company for high-speed travel. Reading about the California high-speed rail was depressing. California taxpayers are paying to build the most expensive high-speed rail per mile in the world—and the slowest. Those are not the superlatives you want.[719]

It's California! We make super high-tech stuff! Why are we spending—the estimates are around $100 billion—for something that will take two hours to go from LA to San Francisco? You can get on a plane and do that in forty-five minutes.[720]

There has to be a better way to do this. What would you ideally want in a transportation system? You want something faster than existing modes of transportation. Let's say twice as fast, costs half as much per ticket, can't crash, is immune to weather, and is not energy intensive. You can self-power the whole thing with solar panels or something. That would be pretty good. The devil is in the details of making the thing work, but something like this could work and be practical.[721]

There's the possibility of this fifth mode of transport; I call it the Hyperloop.[722]

For long-distance travel, you can do tunnels or tubes. If you remove the air or most of the air, you can get rid of the air friction and go supersonic. You can do so with no dependence on weather and no need to get to high altitude or create any sonic boom issues. That's what I envision for the Hyperloop. It's basically a pressurized electric car in a vacuum tube. This will be our next evolution in transport.[723]

We want the future to be better than the past. If we had something like the Hyperloop, you'd look forward to the day that was working. Even if it was only in one place—from LA to San Francisco, or New York to DC—it would be a tourist attraction and show it is possible.[724]

Even if some of the initial assumptions didn't work out or the economics didn't work out quite as expected, it would still be cool. If you come up with a new technology, it should feel like that. If you told a stranger, would they look forward to the day this new thing became available?[725]

Q: What is the most important piece of advice you have for anyone who wants to start a company on behalf of humanity?

The final thing I would encourage you to do is to take risks. Especially before you have kids and other obligations. As you get older, your obligations start to increase. Once you have a family, taking risks affects not just yourself, but your family as well. It gets harder to do things that might not work out. It is easiest to start before you have those obligations. Take risks now, and do something bold. You won't regret it.[726]

> Go do it. Just go out there and do it. People are far too afraid to try. Fear is the biggest reason for failure. Don't be afraid to fail. Just go.[727]
>
> If you don't push for radical breakthroughs, you're not going to get radical outcomes.[728]

COMPANIES DRIVE PROGRESS

> The rate of innovation is not constant. This year, we're either going to increase the rate of innovation or it will slow down.[729]

Some people think technology automatically gets better every year. It does not. It only gets better if smart people work like crazy to make it better. We need strong engineering talent applied to problems. That's how any technology actually gets better. If people don't *work* on technology, it actually will decline.[730]

Look at the history of civilizations and you'll see this happen many times. Ancient Egypt was able to build incredible pyramids and forgot how to build pyramids. Then they forgot how to read hieroglyphics. In Rome, they were able to build incredible roadways, aqueducts, and indoor plumbing—they forgot how to do all those things. There are many examples in history. You should always bear in mind that entropy is not on our side.[731]

More recently, if you look at American manned space missions: We were able to go to the moon in 1969, then the space shuttle could only go to low earth orbit. Then the space shuttle retired and for almost a decade America had no access to space for humans.

This is a pretty bad trend, trending to zero. We need a strong trend in the other direction to have any chance whatsoever of making life multiplanetary. That's the reason for the extreme sense of urgency. If we operate with extreme urgency, we have a chance of making life multiplanetary. Still just a chance; it's not certain. If we don't act with extreme urgency, that chance is probably zero.

I am not one of the doomsday people. I think we're on a good path. But at the same time, I want to caution against complacency. If we are not complacent, and we have a high sense of urgency, things will be fine.[732]

> If you want the future to be good, you must make it so.
>
> Take action to make it good, and it will be.[733]

IF YOU WANT THE FUTURE TO BE GOOD,
YOU MUST MAKE IT SO.

THE AGE OF ABUNDANCE

AI and robotics will bring about what might be termed "the age of abundance."

Other people have used this word, and that is my prediction: It will be an age of abundance for everyone.[734]

THE END OF SCARCITY

People get confused sometimes; they think an economy is money. Money is just a database.

The actual economy is stuff. Goods and services. What limits the output of goods and services? The limiter is labor. Even capital is distilled labor, so the limiting factor for the economy is labor.[735]

We can massively increase labor by building humanoid robots. If you remove labor as the limiting factor for the economy, it's not clear that an economy in the traditional sense has any meaning anymore because you have no constraint on goods and services. There will be no shortage of goods and services.[736]

The first units we intend to make are for jobs that are dangerous, boring, repetitive things that people don't want to do.[737]

In the future, the only forms of scarcity will be artificial scarcity (where we decide to make it scarce, like a particular piece of art) or unique items like a particular home in an exact location.[738]

Don't worry about robots putting people out of jobs. We already have a massive shortage of labor. We will still have a shortage of labor even in the future. Robotics will create a world of abundance—goods and services will be available to anyone who wants them, so cheap it'll be ridiculous.[739]

Our goal at Tesla is to make a useful humanoid robot as quickly as possible. Eventually, there will be millions of them. This means a future of abundance, a future where there is no poverty. We can afford to have a universal basic income for people. It really is a fundamental transformation of civilization.[740]

> People have no idea; the market for humanoid robots will be bigger than that of cars.[741]

There will be humanoid robots throughout factories. Cars will also be entirely automatic. Anywhere intelligence can be applied will be automated. That's maybe 2033–2043.[742]

As we go further into the future, things are gonna change a lot. Everything will be automatic. There will be household robots that you can talk to as if they are people. It will help you, be a companion, or whatever the case may be. It will be able to pick up your kids from school or stay with them at school if you want. It will be able to teach kids anything and support any language.

Long term, I think the ratio of humanoid robots will be more than one-to-one. There might be two humanoid robots per person or more, maybe ten for every one. Well in excess of ten billion humanoid robots. At volume production, a humanoid robot will cost less than a car.[743]

EXPONENTIAL INTELLIGENCE

Computing power is going to be crazy. The big change is the cost of computing power, not so much the circuit density (known as Moore's Law). If you look at dollars per instruction, cost is dropping exponentially.

We'll see massively parallel computers, computing power, and storage become extremely available. There will be ubiquitous computing everywhere.[744]

I expect AI to be incredibly sophisticated by the 2040s. Predicting trends in an exponential curve is tricky, because up close it often looks linear. But actually, it's not linear. The pace of AI development itself appears to be accelerating.[745]

The ratio of total digital compute to total biological compute is the key metric to watch. This is perhaps the most fundamental ratio defining technological progress. It is rising incredibly fast.[746]

We're building progressively greater intelligences, *and* the percentage of nonhuman intelligence is increasing. Eventually we humans will represent a small percentage of total intelligence. It might feel like we're the biological bootloader for AI.[747]

We're fairly close to artificial general intelligence, perhaps only a few years away. It's possible we are on the event horizon of the black hole that is artificial superintelligence. Over a twenty- to thirty-year time frame, things could be transformed beyond belief. We probably won't recognize society in thirty years.[748]

UPGRADING THE HUMAN MIND

The internet is a great leveler for information and education. You can learn anything online for free.[749]

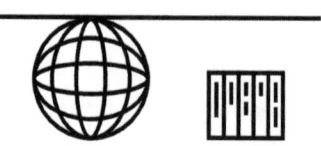

**THE INTERNET IS A GREAT LEVELER FOR INFORMATION AND EDUCATION.
YOU CAN LEARN ANYTHING ONLINE FOR FREE.**

A thousand years ago there were very few books.[750] Even if you had a thirst for knowledge you couldn't do much about it, because books were incredibly expensive and rare, and only a few people knew how to read. Books were difficult to get until the Gutenberg Press. Technology is what causes these big step-changes in civilization.[751]

Even if you could read and were in the Library of Congress, you still didn't have access to all the world's information, and you certainly couldn't search it. And, of course, very few people could be in the Library of Congress at once.[752]

The internet is something beyond the Gutenberg press. When the general public started using the internet, it felt like humanity was developing a nervous system. Any part of humanity got access to almost all human knowledge. You could be deep in the Amazon jungle with a Starlink terminal and have access to more information than the US president did in 1980.[753]

To transfer data before the digital age, you had to write a letter. Someone would have to carry the letter to another person with a bunch of physical work in between. That's insanely slow when you think about it. Now, you can access any book instantly; you can learn anything. It's incredible.[754]

> Any student of history would agree: The internet has been the biggest equalizer in history for access to information and knowledge.[755]

We already have a digital layer to our minds, in a sense, with our computer or our phone. You can access any book or song. You can ask a question on Google and get an answer instantly. With your laptop, you can outcompute an Empire State Building filled with people and calculators. These are incredible superpowers, which even the president of the United States didn't have back in the year 2000.[756]

People don't appreciate this yet—they are already a cyborg. You're a different creature than you would have been twenty years ago, or even ten years ago.

They do surveys asking, "How long can you be away from your phone?" Particularly for younger people, even a day is painful. If you leave your phone behind, it's like missing a limb. People have already merged with their phones.[757]

> You're already digitally superhuman.[758]

Q: Will the brain–computer interface change humans and how we use computers?

Yes, an intertwined idea is having a higher-bandwidth interface between computers and the brain. We're currently bandwidth limited. The connection is bottlenecked in this tiny straw of an interface, poking glass with your meat sticks.[759]

Ten-finger typing on a keyboard used to be the most common

input to a computer. Now, it's usually two-thumb typing. Our output quality has gone backward.

The sustained output of a human over the course of a day is less than one bit per second. There are 86,400 seconds in a day. It is extremely rare for a human to output more than that number of symbols per day, certainly for several days in a row. We should be able to improve that by many orders of magnitude with a direct neural interface—a high-bandwidth interface to your digital enhancements.[760]

Noland Arbaugh was the very first Neuralink patient. After he got the Neuralink implant, he spent all night playing *Civilization*, which is awesome. That's exactly what I'd do too. Even with only roughly 10 to 15 percent of the electrodes working, we were able to achieve a bit per second. That was twice the previous world record. Maybe five years from now, we might be at a megabit—faster than any human could possibly communicate by typing or speaking.[761]

The Neuralink interface can massively increase your output bandwidth and your input bandwidth. Input being written operations to the brain, where the brain is reading signals.[762] If we achieve tight symbiosis, AI wouldn't be "other"—it would be integrated with you. Imagine it has a relationship to your conscious mind similar to your unconscious mind.[763]

Your brain has to work to compress a bunch of concepts in your head into this incredibly low data rate format called speech or typing. That's what language is—a compression algorithm on thought, to transfer a concept. Then it's got to listen and decompress what's coming in. Both of these steps are very lossy.

If you have two direct-brain interfaces, you could do an uncompressed direct conceptual communication with another person. Like consensual telepathy. The conversation would be a conceptual interaction on a level that's difficult to conceive of right now.[764]

> Conceivably, there's a way to have a digital layer of your brain feel like part of you. It's not something you offload to consciously; it's just "you."[765]

To start out, we are really just solving basic neurological damage, like for people who have essentially complete or near complete loss from the brain to the body. For someone like Stephen Hawking, the Neuralink would be incredibly profound. Imagine if Stephen Hawking could communicate as fast as we're communicating, perhaps faster. And that's certainly possible. Probable, in fact.

There's obviously some risk with a new device. You can't get the risk down to zero; it's not possible. So, you want to have the highest possible reward, given there's a certain irreducible risk. And if somebody's able to have a profound improvement in their communication, that's worth the risk.[766]

We can deliver new information to the brain too. If somebody is completely blind, we can write directly to the visual cortex to give them sight. At first it will be relatively fairly low resolution, but long term you would have very high resolution.[767]

This is actually our second product, called Blindsight. It enables people who are completely blind, lost both eyes or optic nerve, or just can't see at all, to be able to see by directly triggering the neurons in the visual cortex.[768]

At some point, the cybernetic implants wouldn't simply be correcting things that went wrong but augmenting human capabilities. You could even see multispectral wavelengths like infrared, ultraviolet, and radar. That's a superpower situation. Augmenting intelligence, senses, and bandwidth dramatically—that's going to happen at some point.[769]

THE LAST HUMAN DRIVERS

It's crazy to let people drive a two-ton death machine manually. They can drive into whatever they want. In the future, it's going to seem like a mad thing that people once drove cars.[770]

In the early days of Tesla, 2013, a guy fell asleep at the wheel in a Model S, and he ran over a cyclist and killed him. Unfortunately, people fall asleep at the wheel often. If we had already built autopilot, this cyclist would still be alive. I thought, *We'd better hurry up and get it working.*[771]

There are clearly two massive revolutions coming to the automobile industry; one is the transition to electrification, and then the other is autonomy. It became obvious to me that in the future, any car that does not have autonomy would be about as useful as a horse. That's not to say it has no use...but it is rare for somebody to have a horse these days. It's obvious cars will drive themselves completely; it's just a question of time.[772]

> An autonomous car is arguably worth five to ten times more than a car that is not autonomous.[773]

The autonomy system is likely to mitigate crashes except in rare circumstances. Vehicle safety is probabilistic. There's some chance any time a human driver gets in a car that they will have an accident that is their fault. The odds are never zero. The key threshold for autonomy is: How much better does autonomy need to be than a person before you can rely on it?[774]

About a million people die every year in car accidents and about ten million per year have serious injuries. Bringing the day of self-driving sooner translates directly to lives saved and injuries avoided. The sooner, the better. A lot of lives will be saved and made better.[775]

Tesla deployed partial autonomy immediately because when used correctly, it was already significantly safer than a person driving by themself. It would be morally reprehensible to delay release simply for fear of bad press or some mercantile calculation of legal liability.[776]

Autonomous cars could maneuver with a reaction time much faster than a human. Over time, autopilot will be capable of impossible maneuvers that a human could never do.[777]

I told the team I want the latest data on miles per intervention to be the starting slide at each of our meetings. If we're training AI to drive, what do we optimize? The answer is higher miles between interventions. It is motivating to watch each day as the miles per intervention increases. Video games without a score are boring.

We always try to do the right thing. When we make mistakes, it may be because we were being foolish or stupid, but it's always with the right motivations.[778]

When true self-driving is approved by regulators, you will be able to summon your Tesla from pretty much anywhere. Once it picks you up, you will be able to sleep, read, or do anything else en route to your destination.[779]

Mega-long-term, I think of cars as being effectively carriers for the autonomy software. It's the vehicle, literally and figuratively for autonomy. It's the software that rides on the car.[780]

Eventually, self-driving cars will take the form of a shared autonomous fleet. You buy your car, and you could choose to use your car exclusively yourself, have it used only by friends and family, or only by other drivers who are rated five stars. You can choose to share it sometimes but not other times. That's 100 percent what will occur. It's just a question of when.[781]

This autonomy shift is massive, because you could suddenly have five times the utility of the car you currently have. Say a normal passenger car gets ten to twelve hours a week of usage. An autonomous car could be used fifty to sixty hours a week.[782]

This is all good for the environment, because you need fewer cars to get the same thing done. We would need fewer parking lots and garages to store cars when they're not in use, because they're in use a lot more.[783]

If this is true, as autonomous driving capability is turned on for the Tesla fleet, it may be the biggest asset value increase in history...overnight.[784]

So, in short, Master Plan Part Deux is:

- → Create stunning solar roofs with seamlessly integrated battery storage.
- → Expand the electric vehicle product line to address all major segments.
- → Develop a self-driving capability that is ten times safer than manual via massive fleet learning.
- → Enable your car to make money for you when you aren't using it.[785]

I can't say enough about the profundity of full self-driving. It will be one of the biggest changes in history. It's not just some feature; it is as profound as electrification. We already have millions of cars on the road now able to achieve this with the right software update.[786]

Eventually, a vehicle must be designed as a clean Robotaxi. We're going to take that risk. No mirrors, no pedals, no steering wheel. This will be a historically megarevolutionary product. It will transform everything. This is the product that makes Tesla a ten-trillion-dollar company. People will be talking about this moment in a hundred years.[787]

SUSTAINABLE ABUNDANCE

> We're accelerating the world's transition to sustainable abundance.[788]

In Tesla's Master Plan, Part 3, the thing we wanted to convey, more importantly than anything else, is that there is a clear path to a sustainable-energy Earth. It doesn't require destroying natural habitats; it doesn't require us to be austere and stop using electricity. We have published a detailed white paper with all of our assumptions and calculations of a clear path to a fully sustainable Earth, with abundance.

In fact, you could support a civilization much larger on Earth. Much more than the current eight billion humans could be supported sustainably on Earth.

I'm often shocked by how few people realize this. Most of the smart people I know actually don't see this clear path. They think there is no path to a sustainable energy future with our current population. Or that we'd have to resort to extreme measures. None of this is true. In Master Plan, Part 3, we walk through the calculations for how to create a sustainable-energy civilization.[789]

A fully electrified and sustainable economy is within reach through the actions in this paper:

1. Repower the existing grid with renewables
2. Switch to electric vehicles

3. Switch to heat pumps in residential, business, and industry
4. Electrify high-temperature heat delivery and hydrogen production
5. Sustainably fuel planes and boats
6. Manufacture the sustainable energy economy

Our models show the electrified and sustainable future is technically feasible and requires *less* investment and *less* material extraction than continuing today's unsustainable energy economy.[790]

The tools we make at Tesla help us build the products that advance human prosperity. Making technologically advanced products that are affordable and available at scale is required to build a flourishing and unconstrained society. It serves to further democratize society while raising everyone's quality of life in the process.

The hallmark of meritocracy is creating opportunities that enable each person to use their skills to accomplish whatever they imagine. Everyone deserves access to these opportunities, and technological growth can help ensure that each of us is able to maximize our most limited resource: time.

OUR EXISTENTIAL RISKS

Don't worry about it.

I mean, worry about it.

Because if you worry about it, ironically, it will be okay.

It will be a self-unfulfilling prophecy.[791]

THIS IS THE BEST TIME TO BE ALIVE

Q: What period of history would you prefer to live in the most?

> Right now. The present is the most interesting time in history—and I read a lot of history.
>
> Let's do our best to keep that going.[792]

I find history fascinating. A lot of incredible things have been done, good and bad. By learning about them, you understand the nature of civilization and individuals.[793]

There's a lot of human history, but most of it is people getting on with their lives. Human history is not a nonstop war and disaster. Those are actually intermittent and rare. If they weren't, humans would soon cease to exist. But historians write more about wars than peace. A normal year where nothing major happened won't be written about much. Most people just farmed and lived their life as a villager somewhere.[794]

Life was tough for most of history. In most of human history, a good year would be one where not that many people in your village died of disease, starvation, freezing, or being killed by a neighboring village. If you only lost 5 percent of your village in a year, that was a good year.[795]

Not starving to death would have been the primary goal of most people throughout history. Just making sure they had enough food to last through the winter and not freeze to death.[796]

> If you judge history from what is morally acceptable today, you'd give everyone a failing grade. I don't think anyone would get a passing grade in morality if you look back to even three hundred years ago.⁷⁹⁷

Q: How does history help you understand the future?

I try to understand the rise and fall of civilizations. I've read a lot of history to discern the facts of what humans did.⁷⁹⁸

We take for granted that "it's always going to be there," but if you study history, you realize civilizations rise and fall.⁷⁹⁹

I was reading about the ancient Sumerians, who were arguably the first civilization. They were the first to develop writing, but eventually they died out. Then, nobody could read their writing at all. They were impressive in their time but they faded out as a civilization. The ancient Egyptians, the same thing. One after another. Ancient Greece had its day. There've been ebbs and flows in the Chinese and Indian civilizations over the eons as well.⁸⁰⁰

Only a tiny fraction of what was ever written in history is available to us now. Probably less than 1 percent. If they didn't chisel it in stone or put it in a clay tablet, we don't have it. There are a few papyrus scrolls that are thousands of years old because they were deep inside a pyramid. The little information we have shows many civilizations rising and falling. It's wild. And the basics of human nature are more or less the same today.

We see patterns for civilizations as they go through a life cycle, like an organism does. A human is a zygote, fetus, baby, toddler, teenager, eventually gets older, and dies. Every civilization goes through a life cycle. No civilization will last forever.[801]

The birth rate might be the biggest single threat to the future of human civilization. Artificial intelligence (AI) gone wrong is a big concern. Religious extremism is a concern. There are quite a few important problems to solve.[802]

We should view our civilization as much more fragile than we think.[803]

We must keep civilization going onward and upward as much as possible and try to minimize the civilizational threats that occur.[804]

WORLD WAR III

I'm not predicting a world war anytime soon. But given enough time, it will likely happen. This has been our pattern in the past. In the last century we had two massive world wars, three if you count the Cold War. It's unlikely that we'll *never* have another world war. We probably will at some point.[805]

Any war is tragic and difficult on a local basis. Then some wars are civilization-ending, or have that potential. Global thermonuclear warfare has a high potential to end civilization, perhaps permanently. But it could severely wound civilization and set back human progress to the Stone Age.

> We want to prioritize avoiding civilizational risks over things that are painful and tragic on a local level, but are not civilizational risks.[806]

Few people alive today viscerally understand the horrors of war, at least in the US.

This concerns me.

Obviously people on the front lines in Ukraine and Russia understand how terrible war is, but how many people in the West understand it? My grandfather was in World War II. He was severely traumatized. For almost six years he was fighting in eastern North Africa and Italy. All his friends were killed in front of him. He would've died there too, except they finally gave him an IQ test. After the test, he was transferred to British intelligence in London.

From the war, he had extreme PTSD (post-traumatic stress disorder). Like next level. He just didn't talk. Ever. If you tried talking to him, he'd just tell you to shut up. He won a bunch of medals. Never bragged about it once, not even hinted at it. Nothing. I found out by searching his military records online.

He knows the horrors of war. He would say, "No way in hell do you want war. Avoid it at all costs." But he died thirty years ago. How many people are alive now who viscerally remember World War II? Not many.[807]

I recommend people read about World War I warfare in detail. It's rough. The sheer number of people who died is mind boggling. There's a saying from World War I, "Young boys who don't know each other, killing each other on behalf of old men that do know each other." What the hell is the point of that?[808]

Something must stop the cycle of reciprocal violence. Something must stop it or it will never stop. Just eye for an eye, tooth for a tooth, limb for a limb, life for a life, forever and ever.[809]

I recommend reading Isaac Asimov's *Foundation* series. The premise is protecting society through a dark age. My guess is there will be another dark age at some point.

I'm not predicting we're about to enter a dark age. But there is some probability that we will, particularly if there's a third world war. We need to ensure there are enough of us, enough of a seed of human civilization to revive civilization and shorten the length of a dark age.[810]

> Asimov's Zeroth Law: Take the set of actions most likely to support the humanity of the future.[811]

REGULATION ACCUMULATION

Be cautious about the gradual creep of regulations and bureaucracy.[812]

Humans die, but the laws they created don't.[813]

The early auto industry was a hotbed of innovation at the beginning of the twentieth century. Many regulations were since added in attempts to protect consumers. The government tends to stand in the way of innovation, even with good intentions. Sometimes they overregulate industries to the point where innovation becomes difficult.

It's crazy how much regulation there is. You can argue and get these things changed, but it takes ages. One of the things we're trying to change is the requirement for side mirrors. Why should cars need them when tiny video cameras can display an image inside the car instead? I met with the US Secretary of Transportation and asked, "Can you change this regulation?" Still, nothing has happened. That was in 2011.[814]

I am incredibly compliant.[815]

We wouldn't be allowed to put cars on the road if we did not comply with the vast body of automotive regulations. If we don't comply with *all of them* we can't sell the car. If we don't comply with *all of the regulations* for SpaceX or for Starlink, they shut us down. My companies are cumulatively overseen by a few *hundred* regulatory agencies.[816]

Once in a while, there will be something I disagree with. If I disagree with a regulation, it's because I believe a regulation meant to do good does not actually do good. I believe it is my obligation to object to a regulation that does not serve the public good. That's the only time I object.

Q: But you typically don't like regulations, correct? We read many articles about you pushing back on the regulators.

Don't take what the media presents as the whole picture. This is not an exaggeration: There are probably 100 million regulations that my companies comply with. There are maybe five that we disagree with.

If you sum up only the arguments I had with hundreds of regulators over decades, it can sound terrible. The media does this without mentioning the 100 million regulations we agreed with. They focus only on the five I disagreed with. People only hear about the five and think, "Wow, this guy's a real maverick."[817]

> **The natural tendency is for the hand of the government to get heavier every year.[818]**

The government told me if SpaceX hired anyone who is not a

permanent resident of the United States I would go to prison. The presumption is that if somebody's not a permanent resident, they might take the rocket technology to countries that would use it to cause harm to the United States. Okay, solid reasoning. I agree.[819]

Then a few years later, the Department of Justice sued SpaceX for failing to hire asylum seekers.

If we hire anyone who's not a permanent resident, we go to prison. Now, we're told if we don't hire asylum seekers, we also go to prison. That seems insane.

We have to work to actively reduce the number of laws and regulations. Otherwise, as more laws and regulations are passed, eventually everything becomes illegal. You get into these Orwellian situations where going left is illegal and going right is illegal. There isn't anything you can do that *is* legal.

That's why the California High-Speed Rail project has built only a tiny section that doesn't even have rail on it, even after spending several billion dollars. California has made almost everything illegal. No one can make progress. This is why we can't build high-speed rail in America. It's illegal.

It's not an engineering failure; it's the regulations.[820]

Something needs to change. Civilization's arteries harden over time and we get less and less done because there's a rule against everything.[821]

Obviously we don't want world wars, but wars can have some silver lining. After World Wars I and II, there were huge resets on rules and regulations. Historically, what has cleared away the cobwebs of regulation has been war.[822]

Regulators and legislators create new rules and regulations every year, but don't put any effort into removing them.[823] Without a cleansing function for rules and regulations, they accumulate every year. This is a problem.[824]

Eventually, we're like Gulliver, tied down by thousands of little strings. You can't move. No single one of those strings is the issue. The problem is there are a million of them.[825] We lose our freedom, one regulation at a time.[826]

UNSUSTAINABLE ENERGY

> Generating sustainable energy is the biggest environmental issue that we face.[827]

I'm much less of a climate alarmist than people might think. But we're running this climate experiment, which we know is pointless because eventually we will run out of coal, oil, and gas. This experiment is not going to last forever. We have to transition to something that is long term because we will run out of hydrocarbons to burn. Let's just not run the experiment.[828]

Long term, most of civilization's energy is going to come from solar. Obviously the sun only shines during the day and sometimes it's cloudy, so we need batteries. Solar will be the main way that civilization is powered long term.

> As long as the sun is shining we'll be fine.
>
> If humanity had to get all of its energy from the sun, it could.

Sometimes people say, "What about clouds?" Here is my response, "Do plants grow?" They grow through a solar-powered chemical reaction. If plants grow, you have solar power.[829]

But between now and then we need to maintain nuclear power. I can't emphasize enough, please do not shut down the nuclear power plants and please reopen the ones that have been shut down. It is total madness to shut them down. Total madness.[830]

I'm in favor of nuclear power in any place not subject to extreme natural disasters. Nuclear power is a great way to generate electricity. Obviously we should not be starting up coal plants and shutting down nuclear plants. It doesn't make any sense at all. Coal plants are a hundred to a thousand times worse for our health than nuclear power plants.[831]

How many people have actually died from nuclear accidents? Practically none. How many people have died from coal plants? It's a very big number.[832]

It's a national security risk to shut these things down. It's not only bad for the climate; it is a national security risk as well. People don't understand that coal power plant emissions cause many deaths every year. They are far more dangerous than nuclear power plants.[833]

The future of energy will be primarily solar with wind. We absolutely need stationary storage batteries because of the intermittency of both solar and wind. There will also be hydroelectric, geothermal, and nuclear—these are all good. Battery cell production is the fundamental rate-limiter slowing down a sustainable-energy future. Very important problem.[834]

We want to move as quickly as we can to a solar electric economy. The faster we get there, the better it is for the world.[835]

> We could probably have a civilization that is a hundred times as energy intensive as we currently have it.[836]

MISALIGNED ARTIFICIAL SUPERINTELLIGENCE

I've never seen any technology grow as fast as AI, and I've seen a lot of technology.[837]

We're quite close to digital superintelligence, which will be smarter than any human at anything. Hopefully they will discover new physics; I think they will. They're definitely going to invent new technologies.[838]

Digital superintelligence is also a potential great filter. I hope it isn't, but it might be.

We must be very careful in how we develop AI. It's a great power, and with great power comes great responsibility. It would be wise for us to have (at least) an objective third party who can go in and understand what the various leading players are doing with AI. Even if there's no enforcement ability, at least they can voice concerns publicly.[839]

> The pace of progress matters a lot. We don't want to develop digital superintelligence too far before being able to do a merged brain–computer interface.[840]

We're on the cusp of an artificial intelligence revolution. For a very long time, we've been the smartest creatures on Earth. That's been our defining characteristic. Now, what happens when there's something way smarter than us?[841]

AI is obviously going to surpass human intelligence by a lot. There's some risk that something bad happens, something humanity can't control after that point. Either a small group of people monopolize AI power, the AI goes rogue, or something like that. It may not, but it could.[842]

If AI superintelligence is linked to human will, particularly a large number of humans, it would be guided to an outcome desired by a large group, because it would be a function of their will.

If our communication bandwidth is too low, our integration with AI would be weak. The AI is going to go off by itself, because we're too slow to talk to or work with. The faster the communication, the more we'll be integrated—the slower the communication, the less.

The more separate we are—the more the AI is "other"—the more likely it is to turn on us. If the AIs are all separate and vastly more intelligent than us, how do we ensure they don't have optimization functions contrary to the best interests of humanity?

We may end up with the choice of either being useless and left behind, or being a pet—like a house cat—unless we figure out some way to be symbiotic and merge with AI. (A house cat would be a good outcome, by the way.)

Q: How do we reduce the risk that AI becomes a "great filter"?

We must build benign AI that loves humanity. It is extremely important to build AI with a rigorous adherence to truth, even if that truth is politically incorrect. My intuition is AI could be very dangerous if you force it to believe things that are not true.[843]

Jeff Hinton invented a number of the key principles in artificial intelligence. He puts the probability of annihilating the human race around 10–20 percent. Mitigating the risks of AI is important.[844] We should be concerned about having AI be vastly beyond us and decoupled from human will.[845]

You get dangerous outcomes when you program AI to be politically correct. Things that may seem relatively innocuous now will not be in the future if AI has immense power.

Take the Google Gemini example, where it refused to produce a picture of George Washington as a white man. In fact, any historical figure would automatically be made diverse because it had been programmed to insist on diversity. That sounds okay at first, but what if the AI has so much power it can actually *enforce* diversity?

It could decide there are too many of one kind of people, and kill people until the diversity amount is what it has been programmed to believe is "correct."[846]

> Mark my words: If we do not program AI to be as truthful as possible, that is where it will go. That is where the danger lies.[847]

Superpowerful AI programmed in this way has severe civilization-level risk. I've seen quite a few technologies develop, but none with this level of risk. Artificial general intelligence (AGI) is a significantly higher risk than nuclear weapons, in my opinion.[848]

The core plot premise of *2001: A Space Odyssey* was that things went wrong when they forced the AI (known as HAL 9000) to lie. The AI was not allowed to let the crew know about the monolith that they were going to see but it also had to take the crew to the monolith. The conclusion of the AI was to kill the crew and take their bodies to the monolith.[849]

The lesson there is: Don't force an AI to lie or do things that are axiomatically incompatible, or mutually impossible. Don't force AI to lie, even if the truth is unpleasant.[850]

Honesty is the best policy.[851] We want to have a maximally truthful AI, even if what it says is not "politically correct." We want it to focus on being as accurate as possible.[852]

I can't emphasize this enough. A rigorous adherence to truth is the most important thing for AI safety. And, obviously, empathy for humanity and life as we know it.[853]

AI mirrors the mistakes of its creators.[854]

AI MIRRORS THE MISTEAKS OF ITS CREATORS.
MISTEAKS

Q: Do you think anyone should be trying to regulate this?

There are regulations around anything that is a physical danger to the public. Cars, communications, rockets, aircraft, and medication are all heavily regulated.[855]

The general philosophy about regulation is there needs to be some government oversight when something is a danger to the public. People often don't understand how slow regulation tends to work. It's slow.[856]

Usually, some new technology will cause damage or death. Then there will be an outcry. Then there will be an investigation. Years will pass. Then there will be an insight committee. Then they get to rule-making. Then there will be oversight, and eventually regulation and enforcement. This all takes years. This is the normal course of new regulations.

Look at automotive regulations. The auto industry successfully fought any regulations on seat belts for more than a decade, even though the numbers were extremely obvious. If you had a seat belt on, you were far less likely to die or be seriously injured. Unequivocally. Eventually, after many people died for years, regulators insisted on seat belts.

This time frame is not relevant to artificial intelligence. You can't take ten years from the point it becomes dangerous. It's too late.[857]

> I was trying to sound the alarm on the AI front for quite a while, but it was clearly having no impact.
>
> I realized we couldn't stop it, so we'll have to try to develop it in a good way.[858]

This is what we are addressing at Neuralink. Our initial goal is to help people who are quadriplegics or tetraplegics be able to operate their phone or computer. There is always some risk in the beginning, because it's new technology. The risk–reward trade has to make sense. If you're quadriplegic and with the Neuralink you can operate a phone even faster than someone with working thumbs, that would be a life-changer.[859]

There are a bunch of other things that could be addressed, like extreme depression or morbid obesity, where people die at age thirty-five. We could literally change the setting in your brain and turn off hunger.[860]

Memory enhancement can help people who have memory problems, which could allow them to function well much later in life. Mental disablement of one kind or another happens to all of us if we get old enough.[861]

Brain–computer interfaces are stunning technology. There may be a way to take the signals from the motor cortex in the brain and send signals to the spine past where the neurons are broken. If so, paralyzed people could move their bodies again.

We may enable people to walk again, which would be wild. Even full-body reanimation. Jesus-level stuff.[862]

POPULATION COLLAPSE

> A low birth rate is a slow death for a civilization.[863]

Most historians overlook the role of low birth rates in the decline of civilizations.[864] Will Durant has it correct in *The Story of Civilization*. A counterintuitive thing happens when civilizations are prosperous for too long—the birth rate declines.[865]

The same thing happened in ancient Rome. Julius Caesar and Augustus saw the problem but couldn't solve it. Rome fell because the Romans stopped making Romans. That was the fundamental issue.

Yes, there were other causes. They had a series of malaria epidemics, plagues, and whatnot. But they had those before, too. It became fatal when the birth rate was far lower than the death rate.[866]

> If the birth rate is below the replacement rate and that trend continues, we will eventually disappear. It's elementary.
>
> At a base level: no humans, no humanity.[867]

IF THE BIRTH RATE IS BELOW THE REPLACEMENT RATE
AND THAT TREND CONTINUES, WE WILL EVENTUALLY
DISAPPEAR. IT'S ELEMENTARY.

Durant looked at one civilization after another, hundreds of them. They all went through the same cycle. When the civilization was under stress, the birth rate was high. But as soon as there were no external enemies or they had an extended period of prosperity, the birth rate inevitably dropped. Every time. I don't believe there's a single exception.[868]

> Population collapse is a real and immediate concern.[869]

Twenty years ago, I noticed birth rates were trending toward being below replacement level in every wealthy country. We always have to be cautious about extrapolating any demographic curve...but if you extrapolate the curves, *if* these trends continue, these countries will dwindle into insignificance. They might completely die out.[870]

It's easy to predict what the population of any given country will be. Just take how many babies were born, multiply that by life expectancy, and that's what the population will be if the birth rate continues to that level. It's very straightforward.[871]

You can see the demographic trends clearly. It's a very slow-moving ship. You know who's going to be an adult in twenty years based on who was born last year.[872]

China had a one-child policy. About 2015 they changed it to a two-child policy, then a few years later they changed it to a three-child policy. The birth rate kept plummeting the whole time. They recently had their lowest growth rate ever. China's birth rate reached 40 percent below replacement. Japan is far along in this. Japan declined by six hundred thousand people in 2021.[873]

The US has been below replacement rates since the early 1970s. The only reasons the population is increasing are immigration and people living longer. People living longer is why the population of Earth isn't plummeting already—but it will.

Q: There seem to be a lot of people concerned about overpopulation. Isn't that more of a problem than underpopulation?

> The biggest myth that exists right now is this "overpopulation" myth.
>
> In fact, we have a population collapse problem.[874]

They are operating on beliefs that were true in the past but are no longer true.[875] These are not subjective matters; you can look at the birth rate. It's an objective number. How many babies were born? There are obvious public records of this information.[876]

I'm pro-environment, but the environmental movement has gone too far.[877] The extremist environmentalists view humans as a blight on Earth.[878]

Environmentalism started out with good intentions but paved

the road to hell. It started to view humans as bad. As a burden on the earth that it couldn't sustain. These views are completely false.[879] Most people in the world are operating under the false impression there are too many people. This is not true. They think that having kids is bad for the environment. It is not.[880]

Earth could sustain a human population ten times the current level.[881] Do a first-principles analysis. How much land area do we need to grow food? How much would that encroach on natural habitats? What's the actual food growing potential? Is there enough water? There's plenty of water because Earth is mostly water—70 percent water by surface area. Desalinization is very inexpensive. There's not a shortage of water, surface area, or energy to grow food.[882]

We need to revive the idea of having children as a social duty; otherwise civilization will just die.[883] I keep banging on the baby drum because declining birth rates have been the source of civilizational collapse over and over again throughout history. Let's try to get this one right.[884]

I've heard people say many times, "How can I bring a child into this terrible world?"

I'm like, *"Have you read any history?!* Because this is a very good time. Things were *way worse* at every other time, ever."[885]

Having children is the most optimistic thing somebody could do. It means you care about and believe in the future.[886] I always encourage my friends to have kids, and I'm happy to see many of them do.[887] Afterward, they thank me. Not one person has said they regret it. Ever.[888]

We are biologically inclined to love and nurture our children. To find it deeply fulfilling. If we weren't, we would have ceased to exist long ago. Take a wolf or some other aggressive creature. When that creature has babies, the mother nurtures them and is tender and caring. We've all evolved to love our offspring. It's a natural thing. And it's a relatively fun thing to do![889]

I had my first kid when I was twenty-nine. As of now, I have twelve kids with three women. Trying to set a good example here—having a lot of kids.[890] I get more joy from my kids than anything else in my life. I'm not saying that's the main reason to have kids, we should have them anyway, but my kids are certainly the greatest source of joy in my life.[891]

> We should increase the population of Earth, not decrease it.[892]
>
> Go forth and multiply.[893]

ASTEROIDS AND COMETS

> A big rock will hit Earth eventually. We currently have no defense.[894]

If you think truly long term, you realize eventually there will be some natural disaster—even if it is not made by humans—that destroys all life on Earth.[895]

Most people are probably aware of Halley's Comet. Slightly under once per century, Halley's Comet comes near us. There are probably many objects, many comets that have long periods we simply don't know exist. There are billions, maybe trillions of objects in the outer solar system. Some of them are super-long-period comets.

For example, when the comet Shoemaker-Levy hit Jupiter, it made a hole in Jupiter the size of Earth. If that hits Earth, that is game over. Dead. Everything is dead.[896]

For all of history, Earth did not have any ability to stop asteroids. Now with Starship we have *some* ability to stop small asteroids. Large asteroids and comets are still a danger.

There's always some risk of this occurring. The probable lifespan of all forms of life is much greater if we're a multiplanet and ultimately a multistellar civilization.[897]

BECOMING MULTIPLANETARY

The window of opportunity is open right now to make life multiplanetary.

We cannot count on it being open for a long time.

We need to take advantage while this window is open.[898]

BECOMING MULTIPLANETARY IS AN EVOLUTIONARY-SCALE EVENT

Deciding what is important through the lens of history is a good way to distinguish what seems important now from what is truly important over the long term.[899]

If we get to Mars and beyond, that will seem far more important in historical context than anything else we do. Things like the Soviet Union will be forgotten or merely remembered by arcane historical scholars. The invasion of Iraq won't even be a footnote.[900]

If you zoom out and look at a long period of time—a four-billion-year history of Earth and the evolution of life itself—there are only about six major milestones. Single-celled life, multicellular life, the differentiation into plants and animals, the transition from ocean creatures to land mammals, and consciousness.

Life becoming multiplanetary also belongs on this list of milestones. It would be at least as important as life going from the oceans to land, probably more significant.[901]

The universe appears to be 13.8 billion years old. Earth is about 4.5 billion years old. In another 0.5 billion years the sun will expand and make life impossible on Earth. If it had taken consciousness 10 percent longer to evolve, it would never have evolved at all. Just 10 percent longer.

> Any species that does not become multiplanetary is simply waiting around until their extinction event, either self-inflicted or external.[902]

The geological history of Earth is long and complicated. There have been many extinction events, not just a few. Read about the great extinction events in the fossil record. If you do, you'll see there have been five major extinctions where 80 to 90 percent of all creatures on Earth died.

In the Permian Extinction, 90 to 95 percent of all species were destroyed. Frankly, that doesn't tell the whole story because most of what remained were sponges, fungi, and things like that. Unless you were a mushroom or a cockroach, you died. Almost no large life survived the Permian Extinction.[903]

This doesn't count the *many* cases where entire continents were destroyed. That happened a lot, but wouldn't count as a major extinction. Yellowstone erupts every seven hundred thousand years or so. That would destroy pretty much all life in North America. At least we'll see that one coming now, thanks to our current technology.[904]

> Humans can cause our own extinction too; other creatures didn't have that option.[905]

I'm a fan of Carl Sagan. He had a great way of putting things: "All of our consciousness, all our civilizations, everything we've ever known and done is on this one tiny blue dot."

People get too trapped in their squabbles among humans. They don't think of the big picture. They take civilization and our continued existence for granted. We shouldn't do that. Look at the history of civilizations: they rise and they fall.

Now there's no geographic isolation. Our civilization is globalized, so civilization rises and falls together. This is a big risk. This should be the most important lesson of history: Things don't always go up.[906]

I'm fairly optimistic about the future of Earth. I don't want people to have the wrong impression, like we're all about to die. Things will most likely be okay for a long time on Earth. Most likely, but nothing is certain.[907]

When I talked to Stephen Hawking many years ago, he thought there was roughly a 1 percent chance of civilization ending in any given century. Even a 1 percent chance of consciousness ending is still too much. It's worth spending a fair bit of effort to ensure we back up the biosphere, or build planetary redundancy. This is important. It's like Russian roulette where ninety-nine barrels are empty. Every century is a click. Click, click, click. Eventually...[908]

Making life multiplanetary is one of the most important things we could accomplish. This will help preserve the light of consciousness.

The probability of consciousness existing for a long time becomes much greater if we're on two independent planets. If something catastrophic happened to Earth, life would still exist on another planet.[909]

Say there was a giant meteor impact, a supervolcano, a massive nuclear war, or some super virus. It might not destroy human civilization, but it could knock us back to a much lower technology level, and then we risk a decline to our extinction.[910]

There are certain things we simply cannot avoid on Earth. Is it within your power or mine to stop World War III? I don't think so.[911]

We may get hit by a comet like the dinosaurs. If the dinosaurs had spaceships, they'd probably still be around. Even if we dodge all of that, the sun will continue to expand and eventually engulf Earth and destroy all life in the solar system.[912]

There's a pretty substantial bifurcation in our future: We're either out there among the stars on many planets or confined to Earth until some eventual extinction.[913]

This is the first moment in 4.5 billion years that it has been possible to extend life beyond Earth.[914]

IF YOU LOVE LIFE, PROTECT IT

I've read a lot of history, including the darkest, worst parts of it. Despite all that, I still love humanity. This is why I care about us becoming a multiplanet species, a spacefaring civilization—because I love humanity. I wish to see it prosper and be happy.[915]

I'm troubled by the question, "Why have we not seen any aliens?" It could be because intelligence, or even just life, is incredibly rare. Maybe we're the only life in this galaxy. We should do everything possible to ensure this tiny candle of consciousness does not go out.[916]

Life on Earth hasn't been around very long, and it can easily disappear. Clearly, we need to extend life beyond Earth and become a multiplanet species.[917]

> If we make life multiplanetary, there may come a day when some plants and animals die out on Earth but are still alive on Mars.[918]

Q: Wouldn't it be better to use all these resources and try to resolve problems on Earth?[919]

About half my money is dedicated to help solve problems like climate change on Earth and half to help establish a self-sustaining city on Mars to ensure the continuation of life of all species.[920]

The point is not to move from Earth to another planet and let Earth die. That's not what I'm saying at all.[921]

To put this into perspective, the amount of resources I'm talking about for making life multiplanetary would be much less than 1 percent of all resources on Earth.[922]

Think of it as resource allocation. Do you think it's worth spending half a percent of Earth's resources to ensure we extend consciousness to Mars and other planets, so that no single event can be the end of our civilization?[923]

Redundancy of life is the defensive reason to go to Mars. But also, going to Mars is the grandest adventure I could possibly imagine. I can't think of anything more exciting, more fun, and more inspiring for the future than to have a base on Mars.

Great and terrible things will happen along the way, just as they happened in the creation of the United States. It will be difficult, and some people will probably die. But it will be incredibly inspiring.

Ultimately, if you care about life on Earth, you should want that life to become multiplanetary and ultimately multistellar. Otherwise you're signing the death warrant for all life as we know it. It's inevitable.[924]

> Think of us being a multiplanet species as taking out insurance for life itself.
>
> Life insurance, for life.[925]

THE GATEWAY TO MARS

What started off as basically a sandbar in the middle of nowhere is now Starbase, Texas. We named it "The Gateway to Mars," because this is where we're going to develop the technology necessary to take humanity, civilization, and life as we know it to another planet for the first time in the 4.5-billion-year history of Earth.[926]

Q: Why Mars?[927]

There are not a lot of options, frankly. Venus is a superheated, high-pressure acid bath. Venus is hell, almost literally.[928] The moon is closer but it doesn't have an atmosphere, has only one-sixth of Earth's gravity, and is missing many key resources.[929] Plus, a Mars base is more likely to survive a conflict on Earth than a moon base.[930]

We could establish a crude permanent base on the moon. That would be the next step up from Apollo. Let's not just go there for a few hours and head back; let's have an occupied science base on the moon. We could build epic telescopes on the moon. They would enable us to see what's going on out there. Maybe we would detect those aliens![931]

When we're out there exploring the galaxy, we might find a whole bunch of dead one-planet civilizations. They just never made it to the next planet. Can you imagine doing archaeology on strange ghost-town planets?![932]

Progress is measured by the timeline to establish a self-sustaining civilization on Mars. That's how we gauge our progress at Starbase.[933]

Occupy Mars, man.[934]

Q: How can we actually get enough stuff to Mars to build a city?

We're now at the point where we can produce a Starship roughly every two or three weeks. Now, we don't always produce a ship every two or three weeks because we are still making design upgrades. But ultimately we're aiming for the ability to produce a thousand ships a year.[935]

Starbase will probably be making as many Starships for Mars as Boeing and Airbus make commercial airplanes each year. This is really an enormous scale of manufacturing, because each Starship is bigger than a 747 or an A380.

Tesla and other car companies are still building far higher volumes of complex manufactured tonnage than SpaceX. That is a way of saying it's achievable. These numbers are insanely high by traditional space standards but they are achievable, because they have been achieved in other industries.[936]

> Starship is the key to preserving the light of consciousness. That's what it's all about.
>
> It may end up being the most important thing that we ever do.[937]

We're hoping to increase the cadence of flights to Mars dramatically with every launch window. Roughly every two years we will dramatically increase the number of ships that go to Mars. Ultimately we will try to get to one thousand or two thousand ships per Mars rendezvous.[938]

We'll need to do a lot of orbital refueling. Orbiting rocket tanker ships will replenish the propellant of the ships that will actually go to Mars. We're aiming to demonstrate ship-to-ship propellant transfer. It's hard to make this not look a bit naughty because it's two ships connecting and doing a fluid transfer.

We would create a propellant depot ship that would look like a huge hot dog. Shortly before going to Mars, Starships would take off with a couple hundred tons of payload from Earth. They would reach orbit with almost no propellant left, then get refilled by the tanker for the journey to Mars.[939]

We need roughly ten thousand missions to get to a million tons transferred to Mars. We think we can do this by 2044.[940] My guess is that it will require about a million tons to build a self-sufficient city, but it might be ten million tons. I hope it's not one hundred million tons. That'd be a lot.[941]

Starship in its final form will probably do well over two hundred tons to orbit each flight, with full reusability and the ability to fly multiple times a day. We plan to launch about five uncrewed Starships to Mars in 2026. If those all land safely, then crewed missions are possible in 2028. If we encounter challenges, the crewed missions will be postponed two more years.

It is only possible to travel from Earth to Mars every two years when the planets are aligned. If Mars is on the other side of the sun, you can't get there. Can't go through the sun.⁹⁴² This increases the difficulty but also serves to immunize Mars from many catastrophic events on Earth.

SpaceX will increase the number of spaceships traveling to Mars exponentially with every opportunity. We want to enable anyone who wants to be a space traveler and go to Mars. That means you, your family, or friends—anyone who dreams of great adventure.⁹⁴³

We want to get to the point where we're sending over a million tons at every Mars transfer window. Then we're a serious civilization. A megaton per transfer window. We can't fly there continuously, so we'd have a gathering of a thousand ships or more.⁹⁴⁴

Eventually, there will be thousands of Starships going to Mars. Imagine an armada of Starships waiting in orbit for the planets to align and then this gigantic Starfleet taking off for Mars.⁹⁴⁵ It will be a glorious sight to see! Can you imagine?⁹⁴⁶

> This is an extremely difficult engineering problem. But no new physics is required.⁹⁴⁷

Q: What's the math on the journey to Mars?

The fundamental optimization is minimizing cost per ton to orbit, and ultimately cost per ton to the surface of Mars. This may seem like a purely mercantile objective, but it is actually the thing that needs to be optimized. There is a certain cost per ton to the surface of Mars where we can afford to establish a self-sustaining city. If we don't get the cost down, we can't afford to do it.

It will cost maybe a quarter of a percent or half a percent of gross domestic product (GDP). That is palatable. A few people going to Mars will not cause some meaningful drop in the standard of living.[948] For less than 1 percent of GDP, we can buy life insurance.[949]

> Starlink internet is what's being used to pay for humanity getting to Mars. I would like to thank everyone who has bought Starlink because you're helping secure the future of civilization.
>
> Thank you.[950]

Right now, you couldn't fly to Mars for a trillion dollars. No amount of money could get any human a ticket to Mars. First, we need to make this possible. But we don't just want to have flags and footprints on Mars for fifty years, like we did with the moon. To pass the great filter of existing only on one planet, we need to truly become a multiplanet species.[951]

BUILDING THE NEW WORLD

> Attendance is not mandatory here. It'll be dangerous and people might die.

Few people will want to go to Mars in the beginning. But for some, the excitement of the frontier exceeds the concern of danger.[952] I think it would be *the* adventure—the best adventure one could possibly go on—to go build a new civilization on a new planet.[953]

Some people seem to think this will be an escape hatch, some luxury resort for rich people. It is not. It's a high probability of death relative to Earth. Long journey. Not great food. A lot of hard work.[954]

You have to spend six months on a rocket with a hundred other people. It will be cramped. Like old ocean voyages, six months packed on a little ship in the middle of the ocean.[955]

It's going to take a while to build a real civilization on Mars. The critical threshold is if the ships from Earth stop coming for any reason, does the Mars City die out or not? That's a high bar. You can't be missing anything.[956]

Imagine you're on a long sea voyage and the only thing you're missing is vitamin C. It's only a matter of time before it's curtains. You've got to have all the things necessary to sustain civilization on Mars, including about a million people.[957]

> I would like to die on Mars...just not on impact.[958]

Some Starships could come back to Earth. We want to offer an option of coming back, but most people who go to Mars will probably never come back to Earth.[959]

Most of the ships we send will probably stay there, especially while colonizing Mars, because the ship itself will be so valuable there. Martians will take apart the ship and use it for raw materials.[960]

Once we get to Mars, there will be a lot to do, and it'll take a while to build it all. We have to build out the industrial base, then the city. First, we build a giant solar panel farm to generate energy. Then a facility to make fuel, oxygen to grow plants for food, and everything necessary to support life.[961]

Ultimately we'll need all these things: power generation, ice mining, mining in general, propellent production, long-duration life support, construction, and global communication.[962]

A fuel plant will create the fuel for the return trips of many Starships. It's mostly going to be oxygen plants, because rockets run on 78 percent liquid oxygen, 22 percent fuel. Mars has a CO2 atmosphere and water ice, which is CO2 plus H2O, so plenty of raw material to make what rockets need: CH4 (methane) and O22 (oxygen). Rocket fuel is easy to create on Mars, and in many other parts of the solar system.[963]

> In the beginning, people would live in glass domes. Over time, we'd terraform Mars and make it like Earth.[964]

Mars is cold, but if we warm it up we'll get liquid water. Mars would have an ocean roughly a mile deep on 40 percent of the planet once we warm it up. That's a lot of water. A lot of the ice you see on the poles is actually dry ice. It's frozen CO2.[965]

Terraforming Mars mostly consists of warming it up. We could warm it up either with solar reflectors in orbit or a lot of thermonuclear explosions.[966]

It sounds crazy, but a series of thermonuclear explosions basically creates an artificial sun. If you're worried that it will generate dangerous radiation, have you stood in the sun? The sun is a giant thermonuclear reactor. Obviously we can stand in front of the sun and not die. We could launch a missile every ten seconds or so. It would be like gigantic thermonuclear fireworks.[967]

> We'd create two little suns, pulsing above the north and south poles.

That would warm the poles up enough that the frozen carbon dioxide (CO2) would gasify. The Martian atmosphere would get more dense, with water vapor and CO2 in the air. In Mars's case, more CO2 in the air is good, because it will create a positive cycle to make it warmer with more liquid water—like Earth's environment.[968]

> Even if you don't go to Mars, you can watch this all happen on TV. It'll be so cool.[969]

What I'm describing may sound crazy, but it is a small fraction of what will ultimately be done, as long as we become a two-planet civilization. Look at the history of shipping technology in Europe. When all you had to do was cross the Mediterranean, the ships were pretty lame—they only had short-range vessels, which couldn't cross the Atlantic.

Without the forcing function of long-range commerce, shipping technology didn't improve much. You could do mostly the same things with ships around the time of Julius Caesar and the time of Columbus. Fifteen hundred years later, ships could still only cross the Mediterranean. But as soon as there was a *reason* to cross the Atlantic, shipping technology improved dramatically. The American colonies were needed for that to happen.[970]

> Reusable rockets are the modern-day equivalent of the first ships that could cross oceans.

> Until you have a breakthrough technology enabling travel, there's no way for entrepreneurial energy to do anything.

Once we build reusable rockets, suddenly the opportunity is immense. We're going to do our best to get you to Mars, and make sure there's an environment there where entrepreneurs can continue building and flourish.[971]

The same thing happened with the first cross-continental railroad in the United States, the Union Pacific Railroad. When they were building the Union Pacific Railroad, nobody could predict Silicon Valley, Hollywood, or California becoming the most populous state in the country. That would have sounded crazy. But then they discovered gold.[972]

> It's incumbent on SpaceX and other organizations to figure out how to get to Mars. Otherwise, nothing else matters.
>
> Once we get there, there's a lot that can be done.[973]

There will be a lot of super exciting things that are hard to predict. After the basic infrastructure is built on Mars, there will be an explosion of opportunity for entrepreneurs, because our new world will need everything from iron foundries to pizza joints. This includes everything you can imagine, like starting the first Italian restaurant on Mars. That would be cool, and somebody's gotta do it.[974]

COLONIZING THE GALAXY

> Earth is the cradle of humanity. We cannot stay in the cradle forever.
>
> It is time to go forth, be out there among the stars. Expand the scope and scale of human consciousness.[975]

The big picture isn't just to back up the hard drive of humanity, but to grow humanity into a true multiplanetary species. Let's establish a regular cargo route to Mars. With the economic driver of interplanetary commerce, there will be resources and incentives to massively improve space transport technology, and then things will go to a whole new level.[976]

Starship is not suitable for going to another star system, but it is a general solution for transport anywhere inside the solar system. Once we have a propellant depot on Mars, we can travel to the asteroid belt, the moons of Jupiter and Saturn, and ultimately anywhere in the solar system. This is huge.[977]

> When space travel becomes as common as air travel, the future of civilization will be assured.

One way to look at the progress of civilization is the percentage completion of each Kardashev level. Kardashev level one is harnessing all the energy of a planet. In my opinion, we've only harnessed maybe 1 or 2 percent of Earth's energy. So we've got a long way to go to complete Kardashev level one.

Kardashev level two is complete when we've harnessed all the energy of the sun. That would be—I don't know—a billion times more energy than Earth? Maybe closer to a trillion.

Then, Kardashev level three would be all the energy of a galaxy. We're pretty far from that. So we're at the very, very early stage of the intelligence big bang.[978]

If we can establish a Mars colony, we can almost certainly colonize the whole solar system. We'll go to the moons of Jupiter, at least some of the outer ones, probably Titan on Saturn, and the asteroids. Once we have an Earth-to-Mars economy as a forcing function, we'll cover the whole solar system.[979]

We have to make Mars work. If we're going to have any chance of sending stuff to other star systems, we need to be laser-focused on Mars. That's our next step.[980]

On a galactic time scale, even with slower-than-light travel, we could colonize the whole galaxy. Even some of the neighboring galaxies. If we get a million years, even with no new physics, could we colonize the galaxy? Absolutely. The entire galaxy.[981]

You are the magicians of the twenty-first century; don't let anything hold you back.

Imagination is the limit.

Go out there and create some magic.[982]

BONUS

THE 69 CORE MUSK METHODS

These were selected as some of the fundamental ideas that make Elon and his companies successful. They have been edited or paraphrased into short, memorable maxims.

1. You are capable of more than you think.
2. It's possible for ordinary people to choose to be extraordinary.
3. You can teach yourself anything. Read widely; talk to experts.
4. Assume you're wrong. Aspire to be less wrong.
5. Internalize responsibility.
6. If we don't make stuff, there is no stuff.
7. Creating products and services creates wealth.
8. A useful life is worth having lived.
9. Don't aspire to glory; aspire to work.
10. Take actions that increase the odds of the future being good.
11. Every day, we either increase the rate of innovation or it slows down.
12. Work on what is just becoming possible.

13. Don't wait for the world to want it. If it should obviously exist, go build it.
14. Build what no one else is building.
15. As you move forward, allies will assemble around you.
16. Prototypes are proof.
17. Start somewhere, question assumptions, and adapt to reality.
18. Reason from fundamentals, not from what others are doing.
19. "The magic-wand number." See the theoretically perfect and work toward it.
20. "Know the idiot index." Understand the cost of components.
21. The Algorithm: Question Requirements → Try to Delete the Part or Process → Simplify → Accelerate → Automate.
22. For critical items, have meetings every twenty-four hours to run The Algorithm and check progress from yesterday.
23. Stay as close to the actual work as possible. Do not separate yourself from the pain of your decisions.
24. All requirements should be treated as recommendations.
25. The only fixed laws are the laws of physics.
26. The best part is no part; the best process is no process.
27. Simplicity creates both reliability and low cost.
28. Find the design necessity of every part and every process.
29. Overdelete and add back the absolutely necessary.
30. Push for radical breakthroughs.
31. Be proactive. You will never win unless you take charge of setting the strategy.
32. A maniacal sense of urgency is our operating principle.
33. A factory moving at twice the speed of another factory is basically equivalent to two factories.
34. Attack the bottleneck. If you have 9,999 things that are working and one that isn't, that one sets the overall production rate.
35. You'll move as fast as your least-lucky or least-competent supplier.

36. Do things in parallel.
37. Give teams one key metric to focus on. Video games without a score are boring.
38. Separating design, engineering, and manufacturing is a recipe for dysfunction.
39. Speed of innovation is what matters.
40. Beat competitors on speed, quality, and cost, not anticompetitive behavior.
41. Test the absurd. When something seems impossible, ask: "What would it take?"
42. Money is not the constraint. Exceptional engineers are.
43. Get everyone thinking like the chief engineer.
44. Get a clear, direct feedback loop with reality.
45. Always be smashing your ego. Ensure ability > ego.
46. Ask, "Is this effort resulting in a better product or service?" If not, stop.
47. Good taste is learnable. Train yourself to notice what makes something beautiful.
48. Physics doesn't care about hurt feelings. Make the rocket fly.
49. Empathy is not an asset.
50. Use simple, clear, humble terms.
51. Go directly to the source of information.
52. When hiring, look for evidence of exceptional ability.
53. Combine engineering and financial fluency.
54. To truly lead the product, lead the company.
55. Lead from the front. Sleep on the factory floor.
56. Physically move yourself to wherever the problem is immediately.
57. All bad news should be given loudly and often. Good news can be said quietly and once.
58. Failure is essentially irrelevant unless it is catastrophic.
59. Fear of failure is the biggest cause of failure.

60. Feel the fear and do it anyway.
61. Double down. Push your chips back in.
62. Work like hell. Like every waking hour. Go ultra hardcore.
63. Make sure you really care about what you're doing—and take the pain.
64. We should not be afraid of doing something important just because some amount of tragedy is likely to occur.
65. When something is important enough, do it even if the odds are not in your favor.
66. Don't ever give up. You'd have to be dead or completely incapacitated.
67. Play life like a game.
68. Go ultra hardcore.
69. Humor is a differentiator.

TIMELINE OF ELON MUSK

This is not comprehensive, and focuses on his entrepreneurial efforts. All ages are approximate.

- 1971 – Born June 28; grew up in Pretoria, South Africa.[983]
- 1984 (AGE 12) – Created his first video game, called *Blast Star*.[984]
- 1989 (AGE 17) – Emigrated from South Africa to Canada, worked odd jobs on farms.[985]
- 1990 (AGE 18) – Attended Queen's University in Ontario.[986]
- 1992 (AGE 20) – Transferred to University of Pennsylvania, studied physics and engineering.[987]
- 1994 (AGE 23) – Completed two internships: Pinnacle research working on high energy density capacitors for electric cars,[988] and a video game company (ironically) called Rocket Science.[989]
- 1995 (AGE 24) – Moved to California. Enrolled in Stanford's physics PhD program, but deferred. Started Zip2, building software for maps, directories, and publishing online.[990]
- 1999 (AGE 28) – Sold Zip2 for $307 million cash to Compaq (who owned AltaVista). Personal proceeds of ~$22 million.[991]

- 1999 (AGE 28)—Started X.com, investing $12 million of his money.[992]
- 2000 (AGE 29)—X.com merged with Confinity (founded by Peter Thiel, Max Levchin, and Luke Nosek) to form PayPal.[993]
- 2001 (AGE 30)—Contracted malaria while on a safari in South Africa. Almost died.[994]
- 2002 (AGE 31)—Sold PayPal to eBay for $1.5 billion. Personal proceeds after tax were ~$170 million.[995] Founded SpaceX.[996]
- 2004 (AGE 33)—Invested $6.5 million in Tesla Motors, leading the Series A.[997]
- 2005 (AGE 34)—Invested millions more into Tesla Motors, leading the Series B.[998]
- 2006 (AGE 35)—Invested more millions into Tesla Motors, coleading Series C.[999]
- 2008 (AGE 37)—Falcon becomes the first privately developed rocket to reach orbit.[1000]
- 2008 (AGE 37)—Invested more than $15 million, the remainder of his net worth, into Tesla Motors, leading the Series D. Became CEO of Tesla.[1001]
- 2012 (AGE 41)—First sale of the new Tesla Model S.[1002]
- 2014 (AGE 43)—Co-founded Astra Nova, an online nonprofit school.[1003]
- 2015 (AGE 44)—First reusable orbital rocket booster landed by SpaceX.[1004]
- 2015 (AGE 44)—Co-founded a nonprofit called OpenAI.[1005]
- 2016 (AGE 45)—Co-founded Neuralink.[1006]
- 2017 (AGE 46)—First Tesla Model 3 delivered.[1007]
- 2017 (AGE 46)—SpaceX achieved world's first successful flight of a reused rocket.[1008]
- 2020 (AGE 49)—First crewed SpaceX flight carries astronauts to the International Space Station.[1009]

- 2021 (AGE 50) — Becomes richest person in the world (for the first time).¹⁰¹⁰ Named *Time* Person of the Year.¹⁰¹¹
- 2022 (AGE 51) — Acquired Twitter (now called X) for $44 billion.
- 2023 (AGE 53) — Founded xAI to advance AI development, competing with OpenAI.
- 2023 (AGE 53) — FDA approved Neuralink for human trials.
- 2024 (AGE 54) — First human receives Neuralink brain implant.¹⁰¹²
- 2024 (AGE 54) — Starship's first-stage booster is caught by launch tower "chopsticks."
- 2025 (AGE 55) — Created a city called Starbase, Texas.¹⁰¹³
- 2025 (AGE 55) — Net worth exceeded $500 billion in October, the first person to do so.¹⁰¹⁴

ELON'S RECOMMENDED READING

> Expose yourself to as many smart people as possible. Read a lot of books.[1015]

BOOKS

(Since there are so many links in this section, you may prefer a digital version. Go to ElonMuskBook.org to get a digital version of this chapter.)

FICTION

The Hitchhiker's Guide to the Galaxy by Douglas Adams

This is in fact a book of philosophy, disguised as a silly humor book. If you read it from the standpoint of "Wow, this is an interesting book of philosophy," it is quite insightful. It hits this point: The answer is easy once you can properly formulate the question.[1016]

It also makes fun of bureaucracy. Earth essentially gets destroyed by a sort of clerical error. Aliens decide they need an interstellar highway and Earth is in the way. They post the fact that Earth needs to get destroyed for this interstellar highway, but of course, it's posted on an alien bulletin board that no one on Earth can access.[1017]

The Lord of the Rings by J.R.R. Tolkien

I know it's cliché, but *The Lord of the Rings* is my favorite series ever.[1018]

Foundation series by Isaac Asimov

I recommend reading the Foundation series. It's about how there's likely to be another dark age, which my guess is there will be at some point. I'm not predicting that we're about to enter a dark age, but that there's some probability we will, particularly if there's a third world war. We want to make sure that there's enough of us as a seed of human civilization somewhere else to bring civilization back and perhaps shorten the length of a dark age.

It's unlikely we'll never have another world war. There probably will be at some point. I'm not predicting this, but given enough time it will be likely because this has been our pattern in the past.[1019]

Dune series by Frank Herbert

The Dune series by Herbert is brilliant. He advocates placing limits on machine intelligence.[1020]

Stranger in a Strange Land by Robert A. Heinlein

I like *Stranger in a Strange Land*, although it kind of goes off the rails at the end.[1021]

The Moon Is a Harsh Mistress by Robert A. Heinlein

The Machine Stops by E. M. Forster

An old story by E. M. Forster, worth reading.[1022]

A Game of Thrones by George R. R. Martin

In my opinion, the best books in recent years are by Iain Banks and George Martin.[1023]

Culture series by Iain M. Banks

Compelling picture of a grand, semiutopian galactic future. Hopefully it's not too optimistic about the outcome of AI.[1024]

Waiting for Godot by Samuel Beckett

Have recently come to appreciate the awesome, absurdist humor of *Waiting for Godot*. We so often wait, without knowing why, when, or where.[1025]

Atlas Shrugged by Ayn Rand

It's a counterpoint to communism and useful as such, but should be tempered with kindness.[1026]

The Fault in Our Stars by John Green

I must admit to liking *The Fault in Our Stars*. Sad, romantic, and beautifully named.[1027]

SCIENCES

If the Universe Is Teeming with Aliens...Where Is Everybody? by Stephen Webb

Read it when it came out. Great book.[1028]

The Big Picture: On the Origins of Life, Meaning, and the Universe by Sean Carroll

Highly recommend anything by Sean Carroll.[1029]

The Skeptics' Guide to the Universe: How to Know What's Really Real in a World Increasingly Full of Fake by Steven Novella

The Selfish Gene by Richard Dawkins

Most people don't realize that the origin of the word meme is from this book by Richard Dawkins.[1030]

Merchants of Doubt: How a Handful of Scientists Obscured the Truth on Issues from Tobacco Smoke to Climate Change by Naomi Oreskes

The same people who tried to deny smoking deaths are denying climate change.[1031]

What We Owe the Future by William MacAskill

This is a close match for my philosophy.[1032]

ROCKET SCIENCE AND ENGINEERING

Liftoff: Early Days of SpaceX by Eric Berger

This book is accurate.[1033]

Ignition!: An Informal History of Liquid Rocket Propellants by John Drury Clark

One of my favorite books for learning space travel.[1034]

Modern Engineering for Design of Liquid Propellant Rocket Engines by Dieter K. Huzel

Structures: Or Why Things Don't Fall Down by J. E. Gordon

A good book on structural design. It is really, really good if you want a primer on structural design.[1035]

HISTORY

Learn the lessons of history so we do not repeat the mistakes of the past.

The Lessons of History by Will and Ariel Durant[1036]

The Story of Civilization by Will and Ariel Durant

The Story of Civilization will keep you occupied for a long time. *The Age of Napoleon* by Will and Ariel Durant is an amazing book.[1037] *The Life of Greece* is incredible.[1038]

The Iliad by Homer (Penguin Classics edition)

Something that's really good as an audiobook is the Penguin edition of *The Iliad*. *The Iliad* was meant to be a spoken poem so obviously lends itself very well to being an audiobook and Penguin did a great job of narration. It's quite engaging.[1039]

The History of the Decline and Fall of the Roman Empire by Edward Gibbon

Read Gibbon's famous book about the decline and fall of the Roman Empire and how they had advanced technology in terms of roads, aqueduct plumbing, and so forth and then they basically forgot about it.[1040]

Catherine the Great: Portrait of a Woman by Robert K. Massie

An amazingly expansive and compelling portrait of an incredible woman. Highly recommended. Yeah, I know what you're probably thinking...did she really f* a horse?[1041]

Storm of Steel by Ernst Jünger

I was fascinated by Jünger's famous book *Storm of Steel*, which was published roughly a hundred years ago, about Jünger's experiences in the first world war. For some reason I'm fascinated by war and history in general. I thought Jünger's book was an excellent firsthand account of World War I. A lesson taken from this book is we don't ever want to do that again.[1042]

Not Much of an Engineer by Sir Stanley Hooker

On War by Carl von Clausewitz

There should be a chapter saying, "If you have a decisive technology advantage, you can actually win with minimal casualties."[1043]

The Wages of Destruction: The Making and Breaking of the Nazi Economy by Adam Tooze

The Fifteen Decisive Battles of the World: From Marathon to Waterloo by Edward Shepherd Creasy

Insightful analysis, ensconced in eloquent prose.[1044]

The Art of War by Sun Tzu

An interesting book I've read many times.[1045]

Benjamin Franklin by Walter Isaacson

Great biography of Ben Franklin by Isaacson. Highly recommended.[1046]

Stalin: The Court of the Red Tsar by Simon Sebag Montefiore

Stalin: The Court of the Red Tsar was one of the few books that was so dark I had to stop reading. If only they'd listened to Lenin's last wish, much tragedy may have been averted.[1047]

American Caesar by William Manchester

Steve Jobs by Walter Isaacson

Explore/Create: My Life in Pursuit of New Frontiers, Hidden Worlds, and the Creative Spark by Richard Garriott

Explore/Create is a chronicle of wonder, and the many wondrous things the future may hold. Richard and I have long shared a passion for space. Perhaps one day our kids will create and play games on a new world![1048]

The Autobiography of Benjamin Franklin

Autobiographies are really helpful.[1049]

Britannica Concise Encyclopedia

Read through the condensed version of the Encyclopedia Britannica; I'd recommend that.[1050]

Destined for War: Can America and China Escape Thucydides's Trap?—A Critical Examination of Historical Patterns Leading to War Between Great Powers by Graham Allison

Well, it's worth reading that book on the difficult-to-pronounce Thucydides's trap. I love war history. I like inside out and backward. There's hardly a battle I haven't read about. And trying to figure out what really was the cause of victory in any particular case as opposed to what one side or another claims is the reason. Both the victory and what caused the war.[1051]

Man's Search for Meaning by Victor E. Frankl

AI AND MACHINE LEARNING

Life 3.0: Being Human in the Age of Artificial Intelligence by Max Tegmark

A compelling guide to the challenges and choices in our quest for a great future of life, intelligence, and consciousness—on Earth and beyond.[1052]

Superintelligence: Paths, Dangers, Strategies by Nick Bostrom

Worth reading *Superintelligence* by Bostrom. We need to be super careful with AI. It's potentially more dangerous than nukes.[1053]

Human Compatible: Artificial Intelligence and the Problem of Control by Stuart Russell

Worth reading *Human Compatible* by Stuart Russell (he's great!) about future AI risks and solutions.[1054]

Our Final Invention: Artificial Intelligence and the End of the Human Era by James Barrat

Our Final Invention is also worth reading.[1055]

Deep Learning by Ian Goodfellow, Yoshua Bengio, and Aaron Courville

Written by three experts in the field, *Deep Learning* is the only comprehensive book on the subject.[1056]

BUSINESS AND ECONOMICS

Screw Business as Usual: Turning Capitalism into a Force for Good by Richard Branson

I liked *Screw Business as Usual* a lot. This approach should be taken to heart by all, as it really is a smart move.[1057]

Masters of Doom: How Two Guys Created an Empire and Transformed Pop Culture by David Kushner

Masters of Doom is a great book.[1058]

The Wealth of Nations by Adam Smith

Adam Smith for the win, obviously.[1059]

Zero to One: Notes on Startups, or How to Build the Future by Peter Thiel

Peter Thiel has built multiple breakthrough companies, and *Zero to One* shows how.[1060]

What's Our Problem?: A Self-Help Book for Societies by Tim Urban

Lying by Sam Harris

I read *Lying* by my friend Sam Harris. Excellent cover art and lots of good reasons not to lie![1061]

The Parasitic Mind: How Infectious Ideas Are Killing Common Sense by Gad Saad

The Parasitic Mind is great. He's got a book on happiness as well, which is also quite good. I'm a big fan of Gad Saad.[1062]

A Woman Makes a Plan: Advice for a Lifetime of Adventure, Beauty, and Success by Maye Musk

My mom wrote a book. ♥[1063]

WANT MORE?

There are many ways to dive more deeply into Elon's ideas. Go to ElonMuskBook.org for bonus chapters, audiobooks, interviews, and more.

You might also appreciate my previous books, *The Almanack of Naval Ravikant: A Guide To Wealth and Happiness* and *The Anthology of Balaji: A Guide to Technology, Truth, and Building the Future*.

If you love the illustrations in this book, created by Jack Butcher, find more of his illustrations and much more of his work at VisualizeValue.com.

To learn about similar ideas, concepts, technologies, companies, and investments, join my email list at EJorgenson.com and subscribe to the podcast *Smart Friends*.

APPRECIATION

There are always more names in the back of the book than there are on the front. Thank you to all who generously gave their time, expertise, wisdom, and skill to create this book.

It's staggering to think how many talented people left their fingerprints on these pages. I'm grateful to every one of you.

Thank you first to Elon, for allowing and encouraging this project. I'm honored by the opportunity to build something around your ideas. I appreciate your trust, generosity, and support.

I am grateful to Naval for writing the foreword to this book. You put into words every hope that I had for the impact this book could have, and it meant the world to me. Thank you for kicking off this writing adventure, supporting this book, and being you.

I am grateful for a fantastic editor in Rachel Jepsen, and the supportive team at Scribe Media, in particular my publishing manager, Emmy Koziak, for her patience and flexibility.

I'm grateful to Dylan Kurt for reaching out and taking on the thousand-and-one tasks that shaped this book and every word in it.

I am grateful to Jack Butcher for lending his immense talents once again. The illustrations and visuals in this book are entirely his. He clarifies and elevates every idea he touches. He's a living example of these ideals. Thank you for taking this project on in addition to all of your own. I appreciate your talent, kindness, and heart.

I am grateful to Sam Teller, John Durant, and Sky King for their unique shows of faith in this project and me personally. You are deeply appreciated for your generosity and care.

I am grateful to all of the fantastic interviewers and writers who created the building blocks of this book. I learned something from all of you, and I appreciate you creating and sharing excellent work.

I remain grateful to my parents for every gift, effort, and sacrifice that put me in a position to create this book. You lovingly built the foundation for everything I ever do, and I'll never forget that.

I am grateful for my wife, Jeannine Jorgenson, for being extremely patient with the amount of time this required. This book wouldn't exist without your wise counsel, positivity, and encouragement. I appreciate all the love and care you bring to our family that allows me to work on quests like this. Thank you for always keeping morale high.

I am grateful for author friends who share their expertise and without whom I'd have more confusion and less laughter: Max Olson, Taylor Pearson, James Clear, and Morgan Housel.

I am grateful to my vast crew of beta readers for their time, opinions, and wise advice. Every one of you made valuable contributions to this book, and it wouldn't be what it is without you. My deepest appreciation for each of you: David Senra, George Mack, Ruchir Jajoo, Amanda Orson, Patrick Finley, Alex Wiekowski, Sky King, Megan Darnell, Chase Ilten, Sean Devine, Sean O'Connor, Travis Stoliker, Brady Kurt, Emma Varvaloucas, Raffi Grinberg, Alec Gewirtz, Danielle Krischik, Rame Adi, Everest Brady, Daniel Doyon, Scott Norman, Mitchell Baldridge, Sam Hinkie, Jimmy Donaldson, and Nat Eliason.

I remain grateful to Naval Ravikant and Balaji Srinivasan for trusting me to create what became *The Almanack of Naval Ravikant* and *The Anthology of Balaji*. Both were life-changing projects that led to this opportunity.

I am grateful to Ivan Edgar Garcia, my assistant who faithfully supported me in creating this book and, by taking on many responsibilities, gave me more time to work. (Shout-out to Athena for making this partnership possible!)

I am grateful to the authors and creators who inspired this book. My drive to create and share this book came out of a deep appreciation for the life-changing impact of similar books, a few of which I'd like to name specifically:

- *Poor Charlie's Almanack* by Peter Kaufman (of Charlie Munger's work)
- *Zero to One* by Blake Masters (of Peter Thiel's work)
- *Seeking Wisdom* (and others) by Peter Bevelin (of Buffett and Munger's work)
- *Berkshire Hathaway Letters to Shareholders* by Max Olson (of Buffett's work)

→ *Principles* by Ray Dalio (and team)

I am grateful for the support of many friends and strangers online who supported and encouraged me throughout this project. My DMs overflow with kind words and eager inquiries. I appreciate every gesture. Your energy helped pull me through the thousand-plus hours it took to create this for you.

ABOUT THE AUTHOR

ERIC JORGENSON writes and podcasts about technology, startups, and crafting a bright future. His blog has educated and entertained more than one million readers since 2014. Eric invests in early-stage technology companies. (Please get in touch to invest or pitch a company.)

He is also the author of *The Almanack of Naval Ravikant*, which has been read by millions of people and translated into forty-plus languages to date, and *The Anthology of Balaji*. He lives in Kansas City with his brilliant wife, Jeannine and son, Archer. Join the author's email list for more good ideas and special projects at EJorgenson.com.

SOURCES

1. Elon Musk (@elonmusk), X (formerly Twitter) account, https://x.com/elonmusk.

2. "Elon Musk: '10X Every 6 Months,'" Farzad, April 8, 2024, YouTube video, 32:28, https://www.youtube.com/watch?v=FPpPTp7FIHY.

3. "An Interview with Young Elon Musk in 2007," PBS Wired Science, June 25, 2015, YouTube video, https://www.youtube.com/watch?v=tqoLRlpROG8.

4. "Elon Musk: Digital Superintelligence, Multiplanetary Life, How to Be Useful," Y Combinator, June 19, 2025, YouTube video, https://www.youtube.com/watch?v=cFIlta1GkiE.

5. Lex Fridman and Elon Musk, "Elon Musk: Neuralink and the Future of Humanity | Lex Fridman Podcast #438," Lex Fridman, August 2, 2024, YouTube video, 8:37:34, https://www.youtube.com/watch?v=Kbk9BiPhm7o.

6. "Elon Musk: Birthrate Might Be the Biggest Threat to the Future of Human Civilization," WELT Documentary, April 15, 2022, YouTube video, 47:49, https://www.youtube.com/watch?v=2WX_mgnAFA0.

7. Lex Fridman and Elon Musk, "Elon Musk: SpaceX, Mars, Tesla Autopilot, Self-Driving, Robotics, and AI | Lex Fridman Podcast #252," Lex Fridman, December 28, 2021, YouTube video, 2:31:47, https://www.youtube.com/watch?v=DxREm3s1scA.

8. "TIME Person of the Year: Elon Musk," TIME, December 13, 2021, YouTube video, 12:42, https://www.youtube.com/watch?v=PbVSZvC7UxY.

9. "Tesla AI Day 2022," Tesla, September 30, 2022, YouTube video, 3:23:00, https://www.youtube.com/watch?v=ODSJsviD_SU.

10. "Elon Musk: Digital Superintelligence," Y Combinator.

11. "Elon Musk on How to Build the Future," transcript, Y Combinator, 2016, https://www.ycombinator.com/library/6W-elon-musk-on-how-to-build-the-future.

12. "Elon Musk's Vision for the Future," Stanford eCorner, October 7, 2015, https://ecorner.stanford.edu/wp-content/uploads/sites/2/2015/10/3620.pdf.

13. "Elon Musk's Vision for the Future."

14. Elon Musk (@elonmusk), "Broad Subject Interview with @DavidFaber," X Spaces, audio, May 16, 2023, https://twitter.com/i/spaces/1RDxlavQqaRKL.

15. Johnny Davis, "One More Giant Leap," *The Telegraph*, August 4, 2007, https://www.telegraph.co.uk/culture/3666994/One-more-giant-leap.html.

16. Fridman and Musk, "Lex Fridman Podcast #252."

17. "Elon Musk Talks Twitter, Tesla and How His Brain Works: Live at TED2022," TED, April 14, 2022, YouTube video, 54:45, https://www.youtube.com/watch?v=cdZZpaB2kDM.

18. Jordan Peterson and Elon Musk, "Dr. Peterson x Elon Musk," X Spaces, audio, July 22, 2024, https://x.com/i/broadcasts/1LyGBgPvoDjJN.

19. "Elon Musk at TED2022."

20. "Elon Musk: Tesla Motors CEO, Stanford GSB 2013 Entrepreneurial Company of the Year," Stanford Graduate School of Business, October 9, 2013, YouTube video, 53:08, https://www.youtube.com/watch?v=MBltc_QAUUM.

21. "Elon Musk in 2009—Charlie Rose Interview," Remembrance of Things Past, originally from August 11, 2009, uploaded March 12, 2020, YouTube video, 29:28, https://www.youtube.com/watch?v=ktkV0N0Oask.

22. "Elon Musk's Vision for the Future."

23. "Elon Musk, Charlie Rose Interview (2009)."

24. "Elon Musk, Charlie Rose Interview (2009)."

25. "Elon Musk: The Future We're Building—and Boring," TED, May 3, 2017, YouTube video, 40:50, https://www.youtube.com/watch?v=zIwLWfaAg-8.

26. Tim Urban, "The Cook and the Chef: Musk's Secret Sauce," *Wait But Why* (blog), November 6, 2015, https://waitbutwhy.com/2015/11/the-cook-and-the-chef-musks-secret-sauce.html.

27. Urban, "The Cook and the Chef."

28. "Third Row Tesla Podcast: Episode 7: Elon Musk's Story: Director's Cut," Third Row Tesla, February 9, 2020, YouTube video, 3:35:03, https://www.youtube.com/watch?v=J9oEc0wCQDE.

29. Musk (@elonmusk), X account.

30. Joe Rogan and Elon Musk, "Joe Rogan Experience #1169: Elon Musk," Powerful JRE, September 6, 2018, YouTube video, 2:37:02, https://www.youtube.com/watch?v=ycPr5-27vSI.

31. "Bill Gates and Elon Musk Interviewed by Baidu CEO Robin Li," Science, Technology & the Future, April 15, 2015, YouTube video, 55:49, https://www.youtube.com/watch?v=6DBNKRYVY8g.

32. "Musk, Stanford GSB 2013."

33. Fridman and Musk, "Lex Fridman Podcast #252."

34. "Bill Gates and Elon Musk," Baidu.

35. "Elon Musk's 2003 Stanford University Entrepreneurial Thought Leaders Lecture," Stanford eCorner, shazmosushi, July 12, 2013, YouTube video, 47:58, https://www.youtube.com/watch?v=afZTrfvB2AQ.

36. "Musk's 2003 Stanford Lecture."

37. "Musk's 2003 Stanford Lecture."

38. "Bill Gates and Elon Musk," Baidu.

39 Walter Isaacson, *Elon Musk* (Simon & Schuster, 2023).

40 "2016 Annual Shareholder Meeting," Tesla, May 31, 2016, https://www.tesla.com/2016shareholdermeeting.

41 "RAW Elon Musk Interview from Air Warfare Symposium 2020," The Space Archive, March 2, 2020, YouTube video, 59:01, https://www.youtube.com/watch?v=sp8smJFaKYE.

42 "Elon Musk, Air Warfare Symposium 2020."

43 "Ron Baron Interviews Elon Musk at the 29th Annual Baron Investment Conference," Baron Capital, January 4, 2023, YouTube video, 1:00:19, https://www.youtube.com/watch?v=E-squeb0YJA.

44 Tim Dodd, "Go Up SpaceX's Starship-Catching Robotic Launch Tower with Elon Musk!," Everyday Astronaut, May 26, 2022,YouTube video, 32:58, https://www.youtube.com/watch?v=XP5k3ZzPf_0.

45 Fridman and Musk, "Lex Fridman Podcast #252."

46 Fridman and Musk, "Lex Fridman Podcast #252."

47 Fridman and Musk, "Lex Fridman Podcast #252."

48 Isaacson, *Elon Musk*.

49 Sriram Krishnan and Aarthi Ramamurthy, "Elon Musk Clubhouse Interview," The Good Time Show, Austin Byrd, January 31, 2021, YouTube video, 1:37:26, https://www.youtube.com/watch?v=4_qxJEsvvSA.

50 Isaacson, *Elon Musk*.

51 Krishnan and Ramamurthy, "Elon Musk Clubhouse Interview."

52 Musk, "Interview with David Faber," X Spaces.

53 "A Candid Interview with Tesla CEO Elon Musk," Vator, August 11, 2010, YouTube video, 18:41, https://www.youtube.com/watch?v=B1h1aG0usIY.

54 "Elon Musk USC Commencement Speech | USC Marshall School of Business Undergraduate Commencement 2014," USC, May 16, 2014, YouTube video, 6:16, https://www.youtube.com/watch?v=e7Qh-vwpYH8.

55 "Candid Interview with Tesla CEO," Vator.

56 Meghan Daum, "Elon Musk Wants to Change How (and Where) Humans Live," *Vogue*, September 21, 2015, https://www.vogue.com/article/elon-musk-profile-entrepreneur-spacex-tesla-motors.

57 Musk (@elonmusk), X account.

58 Krishnan and Ramamurthy, "Elon Musk Clubhouse Interview."

59 Isaacson, *Elon Musk*.

60 "Tesla AI Day 2022."

61 "Tesla AI Day 2022."

62 Musk (@elonmusk), X account.

63 "Elon Musk Offers Advice to Young People," Fox News, April 1, 2025, YouTube short video, 1:15, https://www.youtube.com/watch?v=3gSuepHv4Eg.

64. "Elon Musk on How to Build the Future."
65. "Elon Musk's Vision for the Future."
66. Fridman and Musk, "Lex Fridman Podcast #252."
67. "Musk, Stanford GSB 2013."
68. "Elon Musk Reveals His Knowledge on Aliens, Challenges Putin to UFC, and Predicts WW3," Full Send Podcast, August 4, 2022, YouTube video, 3:12:14, https://www.youtube.com/watch?v=fXS_gkWAIs0.
69. "Elon Musk," Full Send Podcast.
70. "Elon Musk," Full Send Podcast.
71. "Elon Musk," Full Send Podcast.
72. "Elon Musk," Full Send Podcast.
73. "Elon Musk," Full Send Podcast.
74. "Elon Musk," Full Send Podcast.
75. Joe Rogan and Elon Musk, "Joe Rogan Experience #1470: Elon Musk," Powerful JRE, May 7, 2020, YouTube video, 2:00:08, https://www.youtube.com/watch?v=RcYjXbSJBN8.
76. "Elon Musk," Full Send Podcast.
77. Peterson and Musk, "Dr. Peterson x Elon Musk."
78. "Elon Musk," Full Send Podcast.
79. Fridman and Musk, "Lex Fridman Podcast #252."
80. "Third Row Tesla Podcast, Episode 7."
81. Elon Musk and Sam Altman, "Elon Musk and Y Combinator President on Thinking for the Future: FULL CONVERSATION," Vanity Fair, October 8, 2015, YouTube video, 47:53, https://www.youtube.com/watch?v=SqEo107j-uw.
82. "Elon Musk at TED2022."
83. "Tesla CEO Elon Musk (2014)," Auto Bild, November 5, 2014, YouTube video, 34:01, https://youtu.be/FE4iFYqi4QU?t=897.
84. "Elon Musk at TED2022."
85. "Elon Musk at TED2022."
86. "Elon Musk at TED2022."
87. "Interview with Elon Musk: 29 September 2011," The Motley Fool, November 23, 2021, YouTube video, 36:46, https://www.youtube.com/watch?v=bg06ojAR_lE.
88. "Elon Musk Answers Your Questions! | SXSW 2018," SXSW, March 11, 2018, YouTube video, 1:11:37, https://www.youtube.com/watch?v=kzlUyrccbos.
89. "Candid Interview with Tesla CEO," Vator.
90. "Dinner Program: To Infinity and Beyond: Jeff Skoll Talks with Elon and Kimbal Musk (Updated)," Milken Institute, July 12, 2013, YouTube video, 50:39, https://www.youtube.com/watch?v=T55CcN5c5as.

91 Peterson and Musk, "Dr. Peterson x Elon Musk."
92 "Clean Tech Summit 2011: IPO Spotlight with Elon Musk," IBF: International Business Forum, February 3, 2011, YouTube video, 44:34, https://www.youtube.com/watch?v=hTBZGWEzR_E.
93 Musk (@elonmusk), X account.
94 "The Mind Behind Tesla, SpaceX, SolarCity ... | Elon Musk," TED, March 19, 2013, YouTube video, 21:04, https://www.youtube.com/watch?v=IgKWPdJWuBQ.
95 Fridman and Musk, "Lex Fridman Podcast #252."
96 "Elon Musk and Kevin Rose."
97 "The Mind Behind Tesla, SpaceX, SolarCity."
98 Urban, "The Cook and the Chef."
99 "The Mind Behind Tesla, SpaceX, SolarCity."
100 Fridman and Musk, "Lex Fridman Podcast #252."
101 "Musk USC Commencement Speech."
102 "Elon Musk and Kevin Rose."
103 Musk (@elonmusk), X account.
104 "Elon Musk: The Future of Energy & Transport," Oxford Martin School, November 22, 2012, YouTube video, 1:26:18, https://www.youtube.com/watch?v=c1HZIQliuoA.
105 Urban, "The Cook and the Chef."
106 "Future of Energy & Transport," Oxford Martin School.
107 "Future of Energy & Transport," Oxford Martin School.
108 Urban, "The Cook and the Chef."
109 Urban, "The Cook and the Chef."
110 "Future of Energy & Transport," Oxford Martin School.
111 "Elon Musk: Digital Superintelligence," Y Combinator.
112 "Future of Energy & Transport," Oxford Martin School.
113 Urban, "The Cook and the Chef."
114 Isaacson, *Elon Musk*.
115 Isaacson, *Elon Musk*.
116 "Future of Energy & Transport," Oxford Martin School.
117 "Elon Musk's Vision for the Future."
118 Fridman and Musk, "Lex Fridman Podcast #252."
119 Isaacson, *Elon Musk*.
120 "The Future We're Building—and Boring."
121 "The Future We're Building—and Boring."

122. "The Future We're Building—and Boring."
123. "The Future We're Building—and Boring."
124. "The Future We're Building—and Boring."
125. "The Future We're Building—and Boring."
126. Fridman and Musk, "Lex Fridman Podcast #252."
127. Fridman and Musk, "Lex Fridman Podcast #252."
128. Fridman and Musk, "Lex Fridman Podcast #252."
129. Fridman and Musk, "Lex Fridman Podcast #252."
130. Fridman and Musk, "Lex Fridman Podcast #252."
131. Fridman and Musk, "Lex Fridman Podcast #252."
132. Fridman and Musk, "Lex Fridman Podcast #252."
133. "Birthrate Threat," WELT Documentary.
134. Eric Berger, *Liftoff: Elon Musk and the Desperate Early Days That Launched SpaceX* (William Morrow, 2021).
135. Rogan and Musk, "JRE #1470."
136. Isaacson, *Elon Musk*.
137. Joe Rogan and Elon Musk, "#1609: Elon Musk," February 11, 2021, in *The Joe Rogan Experience*, podcast, 3:24:00, https://open.spotify.com/episode/2aB2swgyXqbFA06AxPlFmr.
138. Elon Musk, "I Am Elon Musk, CEO/CTO of a Rocket Company, AMA!," Reddit, r/IAmA, January 5, 2015, https://www.reddit.com/r/IAmA/comments/2rgsan/i_am_elon_musk_ceocto_of_a_rocket_company_ama/.
139. "Bill Gates and Elon Musk," Baidu.
140. "Candid Interview with Tesla CEO," Vator.
141. Fridman and Musk, "Lex Fridman Podcast #252."
142. Fridman and Musk, "Lex Fridman Podcast #252."
143. "Elon Musk: 10X Every 6 Months."
144. Musk, Reddit AMA.
145. "Pando Monthly Fireside Chat with Elon Musk," PandoMonthly, The Musk World, originally from July 17, 2012, uploaded October 27, 2023, YouTube video, 1:03:10, https://www.youtube.com/watch?v=1zzMe-b9ch4.
146. "Pando Monthly Fireside Chat."
147. "Bill Gates and Elon Musk," Baidu.
148. Isaacson, *Elon Musk*.
149. "Bill Gates and Elon Musk," Baidu.
150. "2012: SpaceX: Elon Musk's Race to Space," CBS News, 60 Minutes, December 9, 2018, YouTube video, 14:35, https://www.youtube.com/watch?v=23GzpbNUyI4.

151 Fridman and Musk, "Lex Fridman Podcast #252."

152 Musk (@elonmusk), X account.

153 Hannah Elliott, "At Home with Elon Musk: The (Soon-to-Be) Bachelor Billionaire," *Forbes*, March 26, 2012, https://www.forbes.com/sites/hannahelliott/2012/03/26/at-home-with-elon-musk-the-soon-to-be-bachelor-billionaire/?sh=6926dd2f729b.

154 John Battelle and Elon Musk, "Conversation with Elon Musk (Tesla Motors): Web 2.0 Summit 08," O'Reilly, November 10, 2008, YouTube video, 29:35, https://www.youtube.com/watch?v=gVwmNaPsxLc.

155 Berger, *Liftoff*.

156 Chris Anderson, "Elon Musk's Mission to Mars," *Wired*, October 21, 2012, https://www.wired.com/2012/10/ff-elon-musk-qa/.

157 Anderson, "Elon Musk's Mission to Mars."

158 Urban, "The Cook and the Chef."

159 "Elon Musk, Charlie Rose Interview (2009)."

160 "CHM Revolutionaries: An Evening with Elon Musk," Computer History Museum, recorded January 22, 2013, uploaded February 5, 2013, YouTube video, 1:16:51, https://www.youtube.com/watch?v=AHHwXUm3iIg.

161 "CHM Revolutionaries: An Evening with Elon Musk."

162 Elon Musk, "Elon Musk Commencement Speech at Caltech / CIT 2012," YouTube video, 15:48, posted by "Elon Musk Best Videos," November 22, 2015, https://youtube.com/watch?v=u688eJkLBRM.

163 Urban, "The Cook and the Chef."

164 Urban, "The Cook and the Chef."

165 Musk (@elonmusk), X account.

166 Fridman and Musk, "Lex Fridman Podcast #252."

167 Fridman and Musk, "Lex Fridman Podcast #252."

168 Dan Carlin and Elon Musk, "EP17 Engineering Victory with Elon," Dan Carlin's Hardcore History: Addendum, Dan Carlin, December 13, 2021, YouTube video, 1:41:46, https://www.youtube.com/watch?v=T_Fa50Zc_3Y.

169 Fridman and Musk, "Lex Fridman Podcast #252."

170 Carlin and Musk, "Engineering Victory."

171 Carlin and Musk, "Engineering Victory."

172 Fridman and Musk, "Lex Fridman Podcast #252."

173 Carlin and Musk, "Engineering Victory."

174 Carlin and Musk, "Engineering Victory."

175 Fridman and Musk, "Lex Fridman Podcast #252."

176 Carlin and Musk, "Engineering Victory."

177 Fridman and Musk, "Lex Fridman Podcast #252."

178   Fridman and Musk, "Lex Fridman Podcast #252."

179   Fridman and Musk, "Lex Fridman Podcast #252."

180   Fridman and Musk, "Lex Fridman Podcast #252."

181   Fridman and Musk, "Lex Fridman Podcast #252."

182   Fridman and Musk, "Lex Fridman Podcast #438."

183   "Elon Musk on Advertisers, Trust and the 'Wild Storm' in His Mind | DealBook Summit 2023," New York Times Events, November 30, 2023, YouTube video, 1:33:36, https://www.youtube.com/watch?v=2BfMuHDfGJI.

184   "2023 Annual Shareholder Meeting," Tesla, May 16, 2023, https://www.tesla.com/2023shareholdermeeting.

185   "Pando Monthly Fireside Chat."

186   Musk (@elonmusk), X account.

187   Isaacson, *Elon Musk*.

188   "Bill Gates and Elon Musk," Baidu.

189   "Bill Gates and Elon Musk," Baidu.

190   "Elon Musk," Full Send Podcast.

191   "Future of Energy & Transport," Oxford Martin School.

192   Sal Kahn and Elon Musk, "Elon Musk: CEO of Tesla Motors and SpaceX," Khan Academy, April 22, 2013, YouTube video, 48:41, https://www.youtube.com/watch?v=vDwzmJpI4io.

193   "Elon Musk," Full Send Podcast.

194   "Elon Musk," Full Send Podcast.

195   Musk, "Caltech Commencement Speech."

196   Jimmy Soni, *The Founders: The Story of PayPal and the Entrepreneurs Who Shaped Silicon Valley* (Simon & Schuster, 2022).

197   "Elon Musk, Charlie Rose Interview (2009)."

198   Soni, *The Founders*.

199   Isaacson, *Elon Musk*.

200   Berger, *Liftoff*.

201   Carl Hoffman, "Elon Musk, the Rocket Man with a Sweet Ride," *Smithsonian Magazine*, December 2012, https://www.smithsonianmag.com/science-nature/elon-musk-the-rocket-man-with-a-sweet-ride-136059680/.

202   "Elon Musk Answers Your Questions," SXSW 2018.

203   "Elon Musk: 10X Every 6 Months."

204   Elon Musk, "Elon Musk Commencement Speech at Caltech / CIT 2012," YouTube video, 15:48, posted by "Elon Musk Best Videos," November 22, 2015, https://youtube.com/watch?v=u688eJkLBRM.

205   Krishnan and Ramamurthy, "Elon Musk Clubhouse Interview."

206 Krishnan and Ramamurthy, "Elon Musk Clubhouse Interview."

207 Krishnan and Ramamurthy, "Elon Musk Clubhouse Interview."

208 "Elon Musk on Tesla, SpaceX and Why He Left Silicon Valley | WSJ," The Wall Street Journal, December 9, 2020, YouTube video, 26:47, https://www.youtube.com/watch?v=VlnQFotzQMQ.

209 Isaacson, *Elon Musk*.

210 Fridman and Musk, "Lex Fridman Podcast #438."

211 Noah Magel, ed., *Musk's Memos: The Leaked Emails That Built an Empire* (noah@koda-labs.com, 2024).

212 Isaacson, *Elon Musk*.

213 "Elon Musk: Digital Superintelligence," Y Combinator.

214 "Elon Musk: Digital Superintelligence," Y Combinator.

215 "Elon Musk: Digital Superintelligence," Y Combinator.

216 "Elon Musk: Digital Superintelligence," Y Combinator.

217 Musk, Reddit AMA.

218 "CHM Revolutionaries: An Evening with Elon Musk."

219 "Candid Interview with Tesla CEO," Vator.

220 "CHM Revolutionaries: An Evening with Elon Musk."

221 Rogan and Musk, "JRE #1169."

222 "10 Questions for Elon Musk," *TIME*, July 19, 2010, https://content.time.com/time/magazine/article/0,9171,2002512,00.html.

223 Daum, "Elon Musk Wants to Change How Humans Live."

224 Isaacson, *Elon Musk*.

225 "Elon Musk," Full Send Podcast.

226 Peterson and Musk, "Dr. Peterson x Elon Musk."

227 "Elon Musk," Full Send Podcast.

228 "Elon Musk," Full Send Podcast.

229 Isaacson, *Elon Musk*.

230 "CHM Revolutionaries: An Evening with Elon Musk."

231 Khan and Musk, "CEO of Tesla Motors and SpaceX."

232 Khan and Musk, "CEO of Tesla Motors and SpaceX."

233 Khan and Musk, "CEO of Tesla Motors and SpaceX."

234 "Pando Monthly Fireside Chat."

235 "CHM Revolutionaries: An Evening with Elon Musk."

236 Khan and Musk, "CEO of Tesla Motors and SpaceX."

237 "CHM Revolutionaries: An Evening with Elon Musk."

238 Urban, "The Cook and the Chef."

239 Magel, ed., *Musk's Memos*.

240 Tim Urban, "How (and Why) SpaceX Will Colonize Mars: Part 2," *Wait But Why* (blog), August 16, 2015, https://waitbutwhy.com/2015/08/how-and-why-spacex-will-colonize-mars.html/2.

241 Urban, "SpaceX Will Colonize Mars, Part 2."

242 Rogan and Musk, "JRE #1470."

243 Rogan and Musk, "JRE #1169."

244 Rogan and Musk, "JRE #1470."

245 Musk (@elonmusk), X account.

246 Musk, "Caltech Commencement Speech."

247 "CHM Revolutionaries: An Evening with Elon Musk."

248 Musk, "Caltech Commencement Speech."

249 Musk, "Caltech Commencement Speech."

250 "Elon Musk Talks About His Firing as PayPal CEO 2008," Inc. 5000 Conference, Elon Musk Best Videos, December 4, 2015, YouTube video, 24:50, https://www.youtube.com/watch?v=9e4AaXzagfc.

251 "Tesla AI Day 2022."

252 "Elon Musk: 10X Every 6 Months."

253 "Elon Musk: 10X Every 6 Months."

254 Tim Dodd, "Starbase Tour with Elon Musk [PART 1 // Summer 2021]," Everyday Astronaut, August 3, 2021, YouTube video, 53:16, https://www.youtube.com/watch?v=t705r8ICkRw.

255 "Tesla CEO Elon Musk," *Auto Bild*.

256 Magel, ed., *Musk's Memos*.

257 Jennifer Reingold, "Hondas in Space," *Fast Company*, February 1, 2005, https://www.fastcompany.com/52065/hondas-space.

258 "Elon Musk Answers Your Questions," SXSW 2018.

259 "Musk USC Commencement Speech."

260 "Tesla AI Day 2022."

261 "Tesla AI Day 2022."

262 Magel, ed., *Musk's Memos*.

263 "Elon Musk: 2020 Mars Society Virtual Convention," The Mars Society, October 16, 2020, YouTube video, 56:48, https://www.youtube.com/watch?v=y5Aw6WG4Dww.

264 Magel, ed., *Musk's Memos*.

265 Berger, *Liftoff*.

266 Berger, *Liftoff*.

267 "Tesla CEO Elon Musk," *Auto Bild*.

268 "Elon Musk Answers Your Questions," SXSW 2018.

269 "2023 Annual Shareholder Meeting," Tesla.

270 Battelle and Musk, "Web 2.0 Summit 08."

271 "Third Row Tesla Podcast, Episode 7."

272 "2023 Annual Shareholder Meeting," Tesla.

273 "Third Row Tesla Podcast, Episode 7."

274 "Elon Musk's Vision for the Future."

275 "Jeff Skoll Talks with Elon and Kimbal Musk."

276 Peterson and Musk, "Dr. Peterson x Elon Musk."

277 Isaacson, *Elon Musk*.

278 Isaacson, *Elon Musk*.

279 Isaacson, *Elon Musk*.

280 Magel, ed., *Musk's Memos*.

281 "Elon Musk on Advertisers," DealBook Summit 2023.

282 Magel, ed., *Musk's Memos*.

283 Magel, ed., *Musk's Memos*.

284 Magel, ed., *Musk's Memos*.

285 Magel, ed., *Musk's Memos*.

286 "Tesla Factory Tour with Elon Musk!," Marques Brownlee, August 20, 2018, YouTube video, 15:19, https://www.youtube.com/watch?v=mr9kK0_7x08.

287 "Tesla Factory Tour," Marques Brownlee.

288 Isaacson, *Elon Musk*.

289 Isaacson, *Elon Musk*.

290 Isaacson, *Elon Musk*.

291 Isaacson, *Elon Musk*.

292 Magel, ed., *Musk's Memos*.

293 "Elon Musk: Digital Superintelligence," Y Combinator.

294 "Elon Musk, Air Warfare Symposium 2020."

295 "Elon Musk: 10X Every 6 Months."

296 Tim Dodd, "Talking to Elon Musk and Jim Bridenstine About SpaceX Fly Astronauts for the 1st Time! #DM2," Everyday Astronaut, May 27, 2020, YouTube video, 21:48, https://www.youtube.com/watch?v=p4ZLysa9Qqg.

297 "Elon Musk, Air Warfare Symposium 2020."

298 "Interview with Elon Musk," *Motley Fool*, 2011.

299 "Bill Gates and Elon Musk," Baidu.

300 "Bill Gates and Elon Musk," Baidu.

301 "Bill Gates and Elon Musk," Baidu.

302 "Elon Musk, CEO of Tesla at ONS 2014," ONS: Energy Meeting Place, November 13, 2014, YouTube video, 26:52, https://www.youtube.com/watch?v=0ZsVxSDB7NY&t=2s.

303 Berger, *Liftoff*.

304 "Elon Musk: 10X Every 6 Months."

305 Tim Dodd, "First Look Inside SpaceX's Starfactory w/ Elon Musk," Everyday Astronaut, June 22, 2024, YouTube video, 1:04:17, https://www.youtube.com/watch?v=aFqjoCbZ4ik.

306 Dodd, "First Look Inside SpaceX's Starfactory."

307 Dodd, "First Look Inside SpaceX's Starfactory."

308 Dodd, "First Look Inside SpaceX's Starfactory."

309 Isaacson, *Elon Musk*.

310 Isaacson, *Elon Musk*.

311 "Musk's 2003 Stanford Lecture."

312 "Elon Musk Interview: 1-on-1 with Sandy Munro," Munro Live, February 2, 2021, YouTube video, 48:58, https://www.youtube.com/watch?v=YAtLTLiqNwg.

313 Magel, ed., *Musk's Memos*.

314 Brad Lemley, "Shooting the Moon," *Discover Magazine*, September 8, 2005, https://www.discovermagazine.com/the-sciences/shooting-the-moon.

315 "Third Row Tesla Podcast, Episode 7."

316 "Tesla Factory Tour," Marques Brownlee.

317 "Tesla Factory Tour," Marques Brownlee.

318 "Tesla Factory Tour," Marques Brownlee.

319 "Elon Musk Interview," Munro Live.

320 "Elon Musk Interview," Munro Live.

321 "Elon Musk Interview," Munro Live.

322 "Elon Musk Interview," Munro Live.

323 Fridman and Musk, "Lex Fridman Podcast #438."

324 Dodd, "Starbase Tour, Part 1."

325 Dodd, "Starbase Tour, Part 1."

326 Tim Dodd, "Starbase Tour with Elon Musk [PART 2 // Summer 2021]," Everyday Astronaut, August 7, 2021, YouTube video, 1:01:18, https://www.youtube.com/watch?v=SA8ZBJWo73E.

327 Dodd, "Starbase Tour, Part 1."

328 Isaacson, *Elon Musk*.

329 Isaacson, *Elon Musk*.

330 Isaacson, *Elon Musk*.

331 Musk, "Interview with David Faber," X Spaces.

332 "Elon Musk: 10X Every 6 Months."

333 "Elon Musk, Air Warfare Symposium 2020."

334 Magel, ed., *Musk's Memos*.

335 Elon Musk, "Tesla Battery Day," Tesla, September 22, 2020, YouTube video, 2:11:29, https://www.youtube.com/watch?v=l6T9xIeZTds.

336 "Musk, Stanford GSB 2013."

337 Ashlee Vance, *Elon Musk: Tesla, SpaceX, and the Quest for a Fantastic Future* (Ecco, 2015).

338 "Elon Musk: 10X Every 6 Months."

339 "Elon Musk at TED2022."

340 Dodd, "Starbase Tour, Part 2."

341 "Musk's 2003 Stanford Lecture."

342 "Musk's 2003 Stanford Lecture."

343 Isaacson, *Elon Musk*.

344 "Elon Musk: Digital Superintelligence," Y Combinator.

345 "Elon Musk: Digital Superintelligence," Y Combinator.

346 xAI, "Colossus: Our Gigafactory of Compute," accessed November 14, 2025, https://x.ai/colossus.

347 "Elon Musk Answers All Your Questions (Investor Day 2023)," CNET Highlights, March 1, 2023, YouTube video, 41:03, https://www.youtube.com/watch?v=ZFzhO6fZ9vQ.

348 Berger, *Liftoff*.

349 Chris Anderson and Elon Musk, "Elon Musk: A Future Worth Getting Excited About," TED, April 17, 2022, YouTube video, 1:06:24, https://www.youtube.com/watch?v=YRvf00NooN8.

350 "Elon Musk | Full interview | Code Conference 2016," On with Kara Swisher, June 2, 2016, YouTube video, 1:24:14, https://www.youtube.com/watch?v=wsixsRI-Sz4.

351 "Tesla Motors (TSLA) Elon Reeve Musk on Q1 2016 Results: Earnings Call Transcript," Seeking Alpha, May 4, 2016, https://seekingalpha.com/article/3971543-tesla-motors-tsla-elon-reeve-musk-on-q1-2016-results-earnings-call-transcript.

352 Dodd, "Starbase Tour, Part 2."

353 "Elon Musk Podcast Feb 2019 Full," ARK Invest, Thayqua, February 21, 2019, YouTube video, 29:13, https://www.youtube.com/watch?v=MOy3MTZ9Dyg.

354 "Elon Musk Podcast," ARK Invest.

355 Anderson and Musk, "A Future Worth Getting Excited About."

356 Anderson and Musk, "A Future Worth Getting Excited About."

357 Battelle and Musk, "Web 2.0 Summit 08."

358 "Elon Musk," Full Send Podcast.

359 Rogan and Musk, "JRE #1470."

360 Rogan and Musk, "JRE #1470."

361 Isaacson, *Elon Musk*.

362 Rogan and Musk, "JRE #1470."

363 Musk (@elonmusk), X account.

364 "Elon Musk on How to Build the Future."

365 Elon Musk, "Master Plan, Part Deux," *Tesla Blog*, July 20, 2016, https://www.tesla.com/master-plan-part-deux.

366 "Tesla Q1 2016 Earnings Call."

367 "Elon Musk," Full Send Podcast.

368 "Elon Musk," Full Send Podcast.

369 "Elon Musk, Air Warfare Symposium 2020."

370 Rogan and Musk, "JRE #1609."

371 Dodd, "Starbase Tour, Part 1."

372 Joe Rogan and Elon Musk, "#2054: Elon Musk," October 31, 2023, in *The Joe Rogan Experience*, podcast, 2:41:00, https://open.spotify.com/episode/7edwvm2c6Ieuzun4xtFYCJ.

373 "Elon Musk," Code Conference 2016.

374 Dodd, "Starbase Tour, Part 1."

375 Dodd, "Starbase Tour, Part 2."

376 Dodd, "Starbase Tour, Part 1."

377 Rogan and Musk, "JRE #2054."

378 Musk, "Caltech Commencement Speech."

379 Musk, "Caltech Commencement Speech."

380 "Elon Musk Interview," Munro Live.

381 Rainn Wilson and Elon Musk, "Tesla's Elon Musk Meets Rainn Wilson in the Metaphysical Van Long Before the Cybertruck Was a Thing," SoulPancake, October 8, 2021, YouTube video, 25:11, https://www.youtube.com/watch?v=jMkwsSAIAfY.

382 Khan and Musk, "CEO of Tesla Motors and SpaceX."

383 "Third Row Tesla Podcast, Episode 7."

384 "Elon Musk, Charlie Rose Interview (2009)."

385 "Third Row Tesla Podcast, Episode 7."

386 "Third Row Tesla Podcast, Episode 7."

387 "Third Row Tesla Podcast, Episode 7."

388 "Third Row Tesla Podcast, Episode 7."

389 Musk (@elonmusk), X account.

390 "Third Row Tesla Podcast, Episode 7."

391 "Third Row Tesla Podcast, Episode 7."

392 "Elon Musk's Vision for the Future."

393 Khan and Musk, "CEO of Tesla Motors and SpaceX."

394 "Elon Musk: 10X Every 6 Months."

395 Khan and Musk, "CEO of Tesla Motors and SpaceX."

396 "Third Row Tesla Podcast, Episode 7."

397 Khan and Musk, "CEO of Tesla Motors and SpaceX."

398 "Elon Musk's Vision for the Future."

399 "Elon Musk's Vision for the Future."

400 Khan and Musk, "CEO of Tesla Motors and SpaceX."

401 "Elon Musk's Vision for the Future."

402 "Elon Musk's Vision for the Future."

403 "Jeff Skoll Talks with Elon and Kimbal Musk."

404 "Third Row Tesla Podcast, Episode 7."

405 "Elon Musk: Digital Superintelligence," Y Combinator.

406 "Elon Musk: Digital Superintelligence," Y Combinator.

407 Elon Musk and Maurice J. Fitzgerald, Interactive Network Directory Service with Integrated Maps and Directions, US Patent 5,944,769, filed November 8, 1996, and issued August 31, 1999, https://patents.justia.com/patent/5944769#claims.

408 "Third Row Tesla Podcast, Episode 7."

409 "Third Row Tesla Podcast, Episode 7."

410 "Musk's 2003 Stanford Lecture."

411 "Musk's 2003 Stanford Lecture."

412 "Musk's 2003 Stanford Lecture."

413 "Third Row Tesla Podcast, Episode 7."

414 "Third Row Tesla Podcast, Episode 7."

415 "Musk's 2003 Stanford Lecture."

416 "Third Row Tesla Podcast, Episode 7."

417 "Third Row Tesla Podcast, Episode 7."

418 "Elon Musk Answers Your Questions," SXSW 2018.

419 "Elon Musk Answers Your Questions," SXSW 2018.

420 "Third Row Tesla Podcast, Episode 7."

421 "Musk's 2003 Stanford Lecture."

422 Soni, *The Founders*.

423 "Musk's 2003 Stanford Lecture."

424 Isaacson, *Elon Musk*.

425 "Third Row Tesla Podcast, Episode 7."

426 "Elon Musk: Digital Superintelligence," Y Combinator.

427 "Third Row Tesla Podcast, Episode 7."

428 "Third Row Tesla Podcast, Episode 7."

429 Fridman and Musk, "Lex Fridman Podcast #252."

430 Musk, "Caltech Commencement Speech."

431 Musk, "Caltech Commencement Speech."

432 "Third Row Tesla Podcast, Episode 7."

433 Soni, *The Founders*.

434 Soni, *The Founders*.

435 "Elon Musk: Digital Superintelligence," Y Combinator.

436 Musk, "Caltech Commencement Speech."

437 Urban, "The Cook and the Chef."

438 "Musk's 2003 Stanford Lecture."

439 "Musk's 2003 Stanford Lecture."

440 "Musk's 2003 Stanford Lecture."

441 "The Mind Behind Tesla, SpaceX, SolarCity."

442 Soni, *The Founders*.

443 "Third Row Tesla Podcast, Episode 7."

444 "Third Row Tesla Podcast, Episode 7."

445 "Pando Monthly Fireside Chat."

446 "Third Row Tesla Podcast, Episode 7."

447 "Pando Monthly Fireside Chat."

448 Khan and Musk, "CEO of Tesla Motors and SpaceX."

449 "CHM Revolutionaries: An Evening with Elon Musk."

450 "Musk's 2003 Stanford Lecture."

451 Khan and Musk, "CEO of Tesla Motors and SpaceX."

452 Khan and Musk, "CEO of Tesla Motors and SpaceX."

453 "Musk's 2003 Stanford Lecture."

454 "CHM Revolutionaries: An Evening with Elon Musk."

455 "CHM Revolutionaries: An Evening with Elon Musk."

456 "Elon Musk on His PayPal Firing," Inc. 5000.

457 "Third Row Tesla Podcast, Episode 7."

458 "Elon Musk on His PayPal Firing," Inc. 5000.

459 Max Chafkin, "Entrepreneur of the Year, 2007: Elon Musk," *Inc.*, December 1, 2007, https://www.inc.com/magazine/20071201/entrepreneur-of-the-year-elon-musk.html.

460 "Musk's 2003 Stanford Lecture."

461 "Pando Monthly Fireside Chat."

462 "Musk's 2003 Stanford Lecture."

463 Isaacson, *Elon Musk*.

464 "Future of Energy & Transport," Oxford Martin School.

465 "Conversation avec Elon Musk à Paris 1 Panthéon-Sorbonne," Université Paris 1 Panthéon-Sorbonne, December 3, 2015, YouTube video, 1:03:45, https://www.youtube.com/watch?v=BMskI6G9ty0.

466 Elon Musk, "The Secret Tesla Motors Master Plan (Just Between You and Me)," *Tesla Blog*, August 2, 2006, https://www.tesla.com/secret-master-plan.

467 Musk (@elonmusk), X account.

468 Musk, "Master Plan, Part Deux."

469 "Elon Musk, CEO of Tesla at ONS 2014."

470 "Elon Musk, CEO of Tesla at ONS 2014."

471 "Future of Energy & Transport," Oxford Martin School.

472 "Future of Energy & Transport," Oxford Martin School.

473 "Future of Energy & Transport," Oxford Martin School.

474 Hoffman, "Elon Musk, the Rocket Man."

475 Musk (@elonmusk), X account.

476 Musk (@elonmusk), X account.

477 Anderson and Musk, "A Future Worth Getting Excited About."

478 Anderson and Musk, "A Future Worth Getting Excited About."

479 Anderson and Musk, "A Future Worth Getting Excited About."

480 Musk, "Master Plan, Part Deux."

481 "Elon Musk, Charlie Rose Interview (2009)."

482 "Pando Monthly Fireside Chat."

483 "Third Row Tesla Podcast, Episode 7."

484 "Pando Monthly Fireside Chat."

485 "Pando Monthly Fireside Chat."

486 "Pando Monthly Fireside Chat."

487 "Pando Monthly Fireside Chat."

488 "Pando Monthly Fireside Chat."

489 "Musk, Stanford GSB 2013."

490 "Third Row Tesla Podcast, Episode 7."

491 "Third Row Tesla Podcast, Episode 7."

492 "Elon Musk Interview with Billionaire Investment Legend Ron Baron 2015," Baron Capital, Elon Musk Best Videos, December 4, 2015, YouTube video, 51:05, https://www.youtube.com/watch?v=qsIbGKosY1E.

493 "2016 Annual Shareholder Meeting," Tesla.

494 Isaacson, *Elon Musk*.

495 Musk and Altman, "Thinking for the Future."

496 Musk, "Caltech Commencement Speech."

497 Musk and Altman, "Thinking for the Future."

498 Musk, "Caltech Commencement Speech."

499 Musk, "Caltech Commencement Speech."

500 Isaacson, *Elon Musk*.

501 "CHM Revolutionaries: An Evening with Elon Musk."

502 Musk, "Caltech Commencement Speech."

503 "Elon Musk on His PayPal Firing," Inc. 5000.

504 Musk, "Caltech Commencement Speech."

505 "Talking Tech with Elon Musk!," Marques Brownlee, August 17, 2018, YouTube video, 17:53, https://www.youtube.com/watch?v=MevKTPN4ozw.

506 "Elon Musk, Charlie Rose Interview (2009)."

507 "Elon Musk, Charlie Rose Interview (2009)."

508 Musk, "Secret Tesla Motors Master Plan."

509 Musk, "Master Plan, Part Deux."

510 Musk, "Master Plan, Part Deux."

511 "Young Elon Musk Documentary (1999)."

512 "Young Elon Musk Documentary (1999)."

513 Musk, "Master Plan, Part Deux."

514 "Young Elon Musk Documentary (1999)."

515 "Elon Musk at TED2022."

516 "Elon Musk at TED2022."

517 "Elon Musk: Digital Superintelligence," Y Combinator.

518 "Pando Monthly Fireside Chat."

519 "Pando Monthly Fireside Chat."

520 "Musk, Stanford GSB 2013."

521 Isaacson, *Elon Musk*.

522 Musk, "Caltech Commencement Speech."

523 "Musk, Stanford GSB 2013."

524 Musk, "Caltech Commencement Speech."

525 "Third Row Tesla Podcast, Episode 7."

526 "Third Row Tesla Podcast, Episode 7."

527 "Third Row Tesla Podcast, Episode 7."

528 "Third Row Tesla Podcast, Episode 7."

529 Isaacson, *Elon Musk*.

530 "Elon Musk at TED2022."

531 "Elon Musk at TED2022."

532 "Elon Musk at TED2022."

533 "Musk, Stanford GSB 2013."

534 Musk, "Caltech Commencement Speech."

535 Musk, "Caltech Commencement Speech."

536 Elon Musk, "Elon Musk Writes Letter to the People of New Jersey," CleanTechnica, 2013, https://cleantechnica.com/2014/03/15/elon-musk-writes-letter-people-new-jersey/.

537 "Creating the World's Best Service and Warranty Program," *Tesla* (blog), April 26, 2013.

538 "2016 Annual Shareholder Meeting," Tesla.

539 Musk, "Caltech Commencement Speech."

540 Musk, "Caltech Commencement Speech."

541 Musk, "Caltech Commencement Speech."

542 "The Future We're Building—and Boring."

543 "Elon Musk's Vision for the Future."

544 Musk (@elonmusk), X account.

545 "Elon Musk's Vision for the Future."

546 "Elon Musk's Vision for the Future."

547 "Elon Musk: 10X Every 6 Months."

548 Isaacson, *Elon Musk*.

549 Khan and Musk, "CEO of Tesla Motors and SpaceX."

550 Dodd, "First Look Inside SpaceX's Starfactory."

551 "Elon Musk Delivers SpaceX Update on Starship, Mars Goals and More at Starbase," VideoFromSpace, YouTube video, May 29, 2025, https://www.youtube.com/watch?v=0nMfW7T3rx4.

552 "Talking Tech with Elon Musk," Marques Brownlee.

553 Battelle and Musk, "Web 2.0 Summit 08."

554 "Talking Tech with Elon Musk," Marques Brownlee.

555 Dodd, "Starship-Catching Tower."

556 Musk, "Secret Tesla Motors Master Plan."

557 Musk, "Secret Tesla Motors Master Plan."

558 "Musk USC Commencement Speech."

559 "Elon Musk Interview," Munro Live.

560 Musk (@elonmusk), X account.

561 Fridman and Musk, "Lex Fridman Podcast #438."

562 Fridman and Musk, "Lex Fridman Podcast #438."

563 "2016 Annual Shareholder Meeting," Tesla.

564 "Talking Tech with Elon Musk," Marques Brownlee.

565 "Talking Tech with Elon Musk," Marques Brownlee.

566 Musk (@elonmusk), X account.

567 Musk (@elonmusk), X account.

568 Musk (@elonmusk), X account.

569 Lex Fridman and Elon Musk, "Elon Musk: Tesla Autopilot | Lex Fridman Podcast #18," Lex Fridman, April 12, 2019, YouTube video, 32:44, https://www.youtube.com/watch?v=dEv99vxKjVI.

570 Musk (@elonmusk), X account.

571 "CHM Revolutionaries: An Evening with Elon Musk."

572 "CHM Revolutionaries: An Evening with Elon Musk."

573 "CHM Revolutionaries: An Evening with Elon Musk."

574 "CHM Revolutionaries: An Evening with Elon Musk."

575 "CHM Revolutionaries: An Evening with Elon Musk."

576 Musk, "Master Plan, Part Deux."

577 Isaacson, *Elon Musk*.

578 Dodd, "Starbase Tour, Part 2."
579 Khan and Musk, "CEO of Tesla Motors and SpaceX."
580 *Return to Space*, directed by Jimmy Chin and Elizabeth Chai Vasarhelyi, Netflix (2022).
581 "The Future We're Building—and Boring."
582 Khan and Musk, "CEO of Tesla Motors and SpaceX."
583 Khan and Musk, "CEO of Tesla Motors and SpaceX."
584 "Elon Musk's Vision for the Future."
585 "'Why Does Space Inspire Us?' Elon Musk," SpaceX, December 5, 2011, YouTube video, 1:07, https://www.youtube.com/watch?v=_yDZY5_u8FQ.
586 "Why Does Space Inspire Us?"
587 "Musk, Stanford GSB 2013."
588 Urban, "The Cook and the Chef."
589 "Elon Musk and the Frontier of Technology," transcript, Think Tank with Ben Wattenberg, PBS, December 13, 2007, https://www.pbs.org/thinktank/transcript1292.html.
590 Khan and Musk, "CEO of Tesla Motors and SpaceX."
591 "Elon Musk 'Mars Pioneer Award' Acceptance Speech: 15th Annual International Mars Society Convention," The Mars Society, August 9, 2012, YouTube video, 33:00, https://www.youtube.com/watch?v=PK0kTcJFnVk.
592 Khan and Musk, "CEO of Tesla Motors and SpaceX."
593 Dodd, "Starbase Tour, Part 2."
594 Rogan and Musk, "JRE #1169."
595 "Elon Musk's Vision for the Future."
596 "Elon Musk's Vision for the Future."
597 Khan and Musk, "CEO of Tesla Motors and SpaceX."
598 Khan and Musk, "CEO of Tesla Motors and SpaceX."
599 "Musk, Stanford GSB 2013."
600 "Pando Monthly Fireside Chat."
601 Isaacson, *Elon Musk*.
602 "Elon Musk: Digital Superintelligence," Y Combinator.
603 "Musk Mars Pioneer Award Speech."
604 Isaacson, *Elon Musk*.
605 "Musk's 2003 Stanford Lecture."
606 "2016 Annual Shareholder Meeting," Tesla.
607 "Pando Monthly Fireside Chat."
608 "Musk's 2003 Stanford Lecture."

609. "Musk's 2003 Stanford Lecture."
610. "Musk's 2003 Stanford Lecture."
611. "Musk, Stanford GSB 2013."
612. "Musk's 2003 Stanford Lecture."
613. Isaacson, *Elon Musk*.
614. Berger, *Liftoff*.
615. Anderson, "Elon Musk's Mission to Mars."
616. Anderson, "Elon Musk's Mission to Mars."
617. Isaacson, *Elon Musk*.
618. "CHM Revolutionaries: An Evening with Elon Musk."
619. "Musk's 2003 Stanford Lecture."
620. "Musk's 2003 Stanford Lecture."
621. "Elon Musk: Digital Superintelligence," Y Combinator.
622. "Elon Musk, Charlie Rose Interview (2009)."
623. Khan and Musk, "CEO of Tesla Motors and SpaceX."
624. Berger, *Liftoff*.
625. Berger, *Liftoff*.
626. Khan and Musk, "CEO of Tesla Motors and SpaceX."
627. Berger, *Liftoff*.
628. "Pando Monthly Fireside Chat."
629. Berger, *Liftoff*.
630. Kimbal, "The Plan Going Forward," *Kwajalein Atoll and Rockets* (blog), August 3, 2008, http://kwajrockets.blogspot.com/2008/08/plan-going-forward.html.
631. "ISSRDC 2015: A Conversation with Elon Musk," ISS National Lab, July 8, 2015, YouTube video, 53:03, https://www.youtube.com/watch?v=ZmEg95wPiVU.
632. "SpaceX: Elon Musk's Race to Space," *60 Minutes*.
633. Isaacson, *Elon Musk*.
634. "Elon Musk: Digital Superintelligence," Y Combinator.
635. "Pando Monthly Fireside Chat."
636. Berger, *Liftoff*.
637. Berger, *Liftoff*.
638. Berger, *Liftoff*.
639. Berger, *Liftoff*.
640. "Future of Energy & Transport," Oxford Martin School.

641 Khan and Musk, "CEO of Tesla Motors and SpaceX."
642 "Future of Energy & Transport," Oxford Martin School.
643 Dodd, "Starbase Tour, Part 2."
644 Dodd, "Starbase Tour, Part 2."
645 Dodd, "Starbase Tour, Part 2."
646 Isaacson, *Elon Musk*.
647 Dodd, "Starbase Tour, Part 1."
648 Tim Dodd, "Starbase Tour with Elon Musk [PART 3 // Summer 2021]," Everyday Astronaut, August 11, 2021, YouTube video, 20:51, https://www.youtube.com/watch?v=9Zlnbs-NBUI.
649 Dodd, "Starbase Tour, Part 2."
650 Dodd, "Starbase Tour, Part 2."
651 "Elon Musk Delivers SpaceX Update Following Starship Flight 3! Talk Mars, Moon and More," VideoFromSpace, April 8, 2024, YouTube video, 39:48, https://www.youtube.com/watch?v=7DPR9rzVCzk.
652 Dodd, "First Look Inside SpaceX's Starfactory."
653 "Elon Musk at TED2022."
654 "Future of Energy & Transport," Oxford Martin School.
655 Berger, *Liftoff*.
656 "Elon Musk," Code Conference 2016.
657 "Musk Mars Pioneer Award Speech."
658 "Elon Musk," Code Conference 2016.
659 "Musk Mars Pioneer Award Speech."
660 Tom Junod, "Elon Musk: Triumph of His Will," *Esquire*, November 14, 2012, https://www.esquire.com/news-politics/a16681/elon-musk-interview-1212/.
661 Dodd, "First Look Inside SpaceX's Starfactory."
662 Dodd, "First Look Inside SpaceX's Starfactory."
663 "Elon Musk: 10X Every 6 Months."
664 "Elon Musk SpaceX Update, Starship Flight 3."
665 Fridman and Musk, "Lex Fridman Podcast #438."
666 "Elon Musk SpaceX Update, Starship Flight 3."
667 Dodd, "First Look Inside SpaceX's Starfactory."
668 Dodd, "First Look Inside SpaceX's Starfactory."
669 "Elon Musk's NEW EPIC Rant!," Matt Pocius on Tesla Stock & Money, June 16, 2024, YouTube video, 42:43, https://www.youtube.com/watch?v=dRZUt6tu8bw.
670 "Elon Musk," Code Conference 2016.

671 Peter H. Diamandis and Elon Musk, "Elon Musk on AGI Safety, Superintelligence, and Neuralink (2024) | EP #91," Peter H. Diamandis, March 25, 2024, YouTube video, 30:27, https://www.youtube.com/watch?v=akXMYvKjUxM.

672 Diamandis and Musk, "AGI Safety, Superintelligence, and Neuralink."

673 Fridman and Musk, "Lex Fridman Podcast #438."

674 "Elon Musk SpaceX Update at Starbase," May 2025.

675 "Elon Musk SpaceX Update, Starship Flight 3."

676 "Elon Musk's NEW EPIC Rant."

677 Dodd, "First Look Inside SpaceX's Starfactory."

678 Rogan and Musk, "JRE #1609."

679 Dodd, "Starbase Tour, Part 3."

680 Dodd, "Starbase Tour, Part 3."

681 Dodd, "Starbase Tour, Part 3."

682 "Elon Musk's NEW EPIC Rant."

683 "Elon Musk SpaceX Update, Starship Flight 3."

684 "Elon Musk SpaceX Update, Starship Flight 3."

685 Dodd, "Starship-Catching Tower."

686 "Musk Mars Pioneer Award Speech."

687 Musk, "Caltech Commencement Speech."

688 Musk, "Caltech Commencement Speech."

689 "Musk Mars Pioneer Award Speech."

690 Musk (@elonmusk), X account.

691 Anderson and Musk, "A Future Worth Getting Excited About."

692 "Elon Musk at TED2022."

693 "Jeff Skoll Talks with Elon and Kimbal Musk."

694 "Jeff Skoll Talks with Elon and Kimbal Musk."

695 "Elon Musk at TED2022."

696 "Birthrate Threat," WELT Documentary.

697 "Elon Musk on Advertisers," DealBook Summit 2023.

698 "Birthrate Threat," WELT Documentary.

699 Musk, "Interview with David Faber," X Spaces.

700 "Elon Musk's Vision for the Future."

701 Rogan and Musk, "JRE #1470."

702 "TIME Person of the Year: Elon Musk."

703   "TIME Person of the Year: Elon Musk."

704   Dodd, "Starship-Catching Tower."

705   Wilson and Musk, "Metaphysical Van."

706   Musk (@elonmusk), X account.

707   "Third Row Tesla Podcast, Episode 7."

708   "TIME Person of the Year: Elon Musk."

709   Khan and Musk, "CEO of Tesla Motors and SpaceX."

710   Khan and Musk, "CEO of Tesla Motors and SpaceX."

711   "Tesla AI Day 2022."

712   Musk, "Interview with David Faber," X Spaces.

713   Krishnan and Ramamurthy, "Elon Musk Clubhouse Interview."

714   Krishnan and Ramamurthy, "Elon Musk Clubhouse Interview."

715   "Elon Musk's Vision for the Future."

716   "Birthrate Threat," WELT Documentary.

717   Krishnan and Ramamurthy, "Elon Musk Clubhouse Interview."

718   Krishnan and Ramamurthy, "Elon Musk Clubhouse Interview."

719   Khan and Musk, "CEO of Tesla Motors and SpaceX."

720   Khan and Musk, "CEO of Tesla Motors and SpaceX."

721   Khan and Musk, "CEO of Tesla Motors and SpaceX."

722   "Future of Energy & Transport," Oxford Martin School.

723   "Elon Musk on Tesla, SpaceX," *WSJ*.

724   Khan and Musk, "CEO of Tesla Motors and SpaceX."

725   Khan and Musk, "CEO of Tesla Motors and SpaceX."

726   "Musk USC Commencement Speech."

727   "Musk USC Commencement Speech."

728   "Elon Musk, Air Warfare Symposium 2020."

729   Dodd, "Starbase Tour, Part 3."

730   "Elon Musk on How to Build the Future."

731   "Elon Musk on How to Build the Future."

732   Anderson and Musk, "A Future Worth Getting Excited About."

733   Anderson and Musk, "A Future Worth Getting Excited About."

734   "Elon Musk at TED2022."

735   "Birthrate Threat," WELT Documentary.

736. "Birthrate Threat," WELT Documentary.
737. Anderson and Musk, "A Future Worth Getting Excited About."
738. "Birthrate Threat," WELT Documentary.
739. "Elon Musk at TED2022."
740. Isaacson, *Elon Musk*.
741. Anderson and Musk, "A Future Worth Getting Excited About."
742. Ryan Knutson, "Elon Musk on 2024 Politics, Succession Plans and Whether AI Will Annihilate Humanity," *The Journal*, podcast, May 24, 2023, 18:55, https://open.spotify.com/episode/7HyKBExI7aM0KAGZ6WzmgD?context=spotify:show:0KxdEdeY2Wb3zr28dMlQva&nd=1.
743. "Elon Musk's NEW EPIC Rant."
744. "Elon Musk's Vision for the Future."
745. "Elon Musk's Vision for the Future."
746. Musk (@elonmusk), X account.
747. Rogan and Musk, "JRE #1169."
748. Knutson, "Elon Musk on 2024 Politics."
749. Berger, *Liftoff*.
750. "Tesla AI Day 2022."
751. "Elon Musk (Full Interview) | Real Time with Bill Maher (HBO)," Real Time with Bill Maher, April 29, 2023, YouTube video, 21:20, https://www.youtube.com/watch?v=oO8w6XcXJUs.
752. "Tesla AI Day 2022."
753. "Elon Musk," *Real Time with Bill Maher*.
754. "Tesla AI Day 2022."
755. "Tesla AI Day 2022."
756. Tim Urban, "Neuralink and the Brain's Magical Future," *Wait But Why* (blog), April 20, 2017, https://waitbutwhy.com/2017/04/neuralink.html.
757. Urban, "Neuralink and the Brain's Magical Future."
758. Urban, "Neuralink and the Brain's Magical Future."
759. "Elon Musk on How to Build the Future."
760. Urban, "Neuralink and the Brain's Magical Future."
761. "Elon Musk's NEW EPIC Rant."
762. "Elon Musk: Digital Superintelligence," Y Combinator.
763. Urban, "Neuralink and the Brain's Magical Future."
764. Urban, "Neuralink and the Brain's Magical Future."
765. Urban, "Neuralink and the Brain's Magical Future."
766. Fridman and Musk, "Lex Fridman Podcast #438."

767 "Elon Musk: Digital Superintelligence," Y Combinator.

768 Fridman and Musk, "Lex Fridman Podcast #438."

769 "Elon Musk: Digital Superintelligence," Y Combinator.

770 Fridman and Musk, "Lex Fridman Podcast #18."

771 "Elon Musk," Full Send Podcast.

772 Fridman and Musk, "Lex Fridman Podcast #18."

773 Fridman and Musk, "Lex Fridman Podcast #18."

774 "The Future We're Building—and Boring."

775 Krishnan and Ramamurthy, "Elon Musk Clubhouse Interview."

776 Musk, "Master Plan, Part Deux."

777 Fridman and Musk, "Lex Fridman Podcast #252."

778 "2016 Annual Shareholder Meeting," Tesla.

779 Musk, "Master Plan, Part Deux."

780 "Elon Musk Podcast," ARK Invest.

781 "The Future We're Building—and Boring."

782 "The Future We're Building—and Boring."

783 Krishnan and Ramamurthy, "Elon Musk Clubhouse Interview."

784 "Elon Musk, Investor Day 2023."

785 Musk, "Master Plan, Part Deux."

786 "2023 Annual Shareholder Meeting," Tesla.

787 Isaacson, *Elon Musk*.

788 The Tesla Team, *Master Plan Part IV* (Tesla, September 1, 2025), https://digitalassets.tesla.com/tesla-contents/image/upload/Tesla-Master-Plan-Part-4.pdf.

789 "Elon Musk's Tesla Master Plan 3 in 22 Mins (SUPERCUT)," Farzad, March 2, 2023, YouTube video, 22:48, https://www.youtube.com/watch?v=BoGNEZF2XFQ.

790 Tesla Contributors and Advisors, *Master Plan Part 3: Sustainable Energy for All of Earth* (Tesla, April 5, 2023), https://www.tesla.com/ns_videos/Tesla-Master-Plan-Part-3.pdf.

791 Anderson and Musk, "A Future Worth Getting Excited About."

792 "Tesla AI Day 2022."

793 Fridman and Musk, "Lex Fridman Podcast #252."

794 Fridman and Musk, "Lex Fridman Podcast #252."

795 Fridman and Musk, "Lex Fridman Podcast #252."

796 Fridman and Musk, "Lex Fridman Podcast #252."

797 Fridman and Musk, "Lex Fridman Podcast #252."

798 Peterson and Musk, "Dr. Peterson x Elon Musk."

799 "Elon Musk: 10X Every 6 Months."

800 "Elon Musk: 10X Every 6 Months."

801 Fridman and Musk, "Lex Fridman Podcast #438."

802 "Birthrate Threat," WELT Documentary.

803 "Elon Musk: 10X Every 6 Months."

804 "Elon Musk: 10X Every 6 Months."

805 "Elon Musk Answers Your Questions," SXSW 2018.

806 Lex Fridman and Elon Musk, "Elon Musk: War, AI, Aliens, Politics, Physics, Video Games, and Humanity | Lex Fridman Podcast #400," Lex Fridman, November 9, 2023, YouTube video, 2:16:46, https://www.youtube.com/watch?v=JN3KPFbWCy8.

807 Fridman and Musk, "Lex Fridman Podcast #400."

808 Fridman and Musk, "Lex Fridman Podcast #400."

809 Fridman and Musk, "Lex Fridman Podcast #400."

810 "Elon Musk Answers Your Questions," SXSW 2018.

811 "Elon Musk Answers Your Questions," SXSW 2018.

812 "Elon Musk on Tesla, SpaceX," *WSJ*.

813 Fridman and Musk, "Lex Fridman Podcast #252."

814 "CHM Revolutionaries: An Evening with Elon Musk."

815 "Elon Musk on Advertisers," DealBook Summit 2023.

816 "Elon Musk on Advertisers," DealBook Summit 2023.

817 "Elon Musk on Advertisers," DealBook Summit 2023.

818 Peterson and Musk, "Dr. Peterson x Elon Musk."

819 Peterson and Musk, "Dr. Peterson x Elon Musk."

820 Fridman and Musk, "Lex Fridman Podcast #438."

821 Fridman and Musk, "Lex Fridman Podcast #252."

822 Fridman and Musk, "Lex Fridman Podcast #438."

823 "Elon Musk on Tesla, SpaceX," *WSJ*.

824 Fridman and Musk, "Lex Fridman Podcast #252."

825 Fridman and Musk, "Lex Fridman Podcast #438."

826 "CHM Revolutionaries: An Evening with Elon Musk."

827 "Jeff Skoll Talks with Elon and Kimbal Musk."

828 "Birthrate Threat," WELT Documentary.

829 "Birthrate Threat," WELT Documentary.

830 "Birthrate Threat," WELT Documentary.
831 Fridman and Musk, "Lex Fridman Podcast #252."
832 Fridman and Musk, "Lex Fridman Podcast #252."
833 "Birthrate Threat," WELT Documentary.
834 Musk (@elonmusk), X account.
835 "Birthrate Threat," WELT Documentary.
836 Musk, "Caltech Commencement Speech."
837 Diamandis and Musk, "AGI Safety, Superintelligence, and Neuralink."
838 "Elon Musk: Digital Superintelligence," Y Combinator.
839 Fridman and Musk, "Lex Fridman Podcast #400."
840 Urban, "Neuralink and the Brain's Magical Future."
841 Rogan and Musk, "JRE #2054."
842 Urban, "Neuralink and the Brain's Magical Future."
843 "Elon Musk: Digital Superintelligence," Y Combinator.
844 Fridman and Musk, "Lex Fridman Podcast #438."
845 Rogan and Musk, "JRE #1470."
846 "Elon Musk: 10X Every 6 Months."
847 "Elon Musk: 10X Every 6 Months."
848 Musk (@elonmusk), X account.
849 Diamandis and Musk, "AGI Safety, Superintelligence, and Neuralink."
850 Diamandis and Musk, "AGI Safety, Superintelligence, and Neuralink."
851 Musk (@elonmusk), X account.
852 Diamandis and Musk, "AGI Safety, Superintelligence, and Neuralink."
853 "Elon Musk: Digital Superintelligence," Y Combinator.
854 Musk (@elonmusk), X account.
855 "Elon Musk on Advertisers," DealBook Summit 2023.
856 Rogan and Musk, "JRE #1169."
857 Rogan and Musk, "JRE #1169."
858 Urban, "Neuralink and the Brain's Magical Future."
859 "Elon Musk," Full Send Podcast.
860 "Elon Musk," Full Send Podcast.
861 Urban, "Neuralink and the Brain's Magical Future."
862 "Elon Musk," Full Send Podcast.

863 "Elon Musk," Full Send Podcast.

864 "Elon Musk on How to Save the Human Race at #2024 Milken Conference," Electron media group, inc., May 7, 2024, YouTube video, 40:34, https://www.youtube.com/watch?v=s5o5m7LP6YY.

865 Fridman and Musk, "Lex Fridman Podcast #438."

866 Fridman and Musk, "Lex Fridman Podcast #438."

867 Fridman and Musk, "Lex Fridman Podcast #438."

868 Fridman and Musk, "Lex Fridman Podcast #438."

869 Fridman and Musk, "Lex Fridman Podcast #438."

870 Peterson and Musk, "Dr. Peterson x Elon Musk."

871 Peterson and Musk, "Dr. Peterson x Elon Musk."

872 "Elon Musk on How to Save the Human Race," Milken Conference.

873 "Elon Musk," Full Send Podcast.

874 "Elon Musk," Full Send Podcast.

875 "Elon Musk," Full Send Podcast.

876 "Elon Musk," Full Send Podcast.

877 "Elon Musk," Full Send Podcast.

878 Peterson and Musk, "Dr. Peterson x Elon Musk."

879 Peterson and Musk, "Dr. Peterson x Elon Musk."

880 Musk, "Caltech Commencement Speech."

881 "Birthrate Threat," WELT Documentary.

882 Peterson and Musk, "Dr. Peterson x Elon Musk."

883 Isaacson, *Elon Musk*.

884 Fridman and Musk, "Lex Fridman Podcast #438."

885 Musk, "Caltech Commencement Speech."

886 Peterson and Musk, "Dr. Peterson x Elon Musk."

887 "Elon Musk's NEW EPIC Rant."

888 Peterson and Musk, "Dr. Peterson x Elon Musk."

889 Peterson and Musk, "Dr. Peterson x Elon Musk."

890 "Elon Musk," Full Send Podcast.

891 "Elon Musk on How to Save the Human Race," Milken Conference.

892 Peterson and Musk, "Dr. Peterson x Elon Musk."

893 Fridman and Musk, "Lex Fridman Podcast #438."

894 Musk (@elonmusk), X account.

895. Dodd, "Starship-Catching Tower."
896. Dodd, "Starship-Catching Tower."
897. Dodd, "Starship-Catching Tower."
898. *Return to Space.*
899. "Elon Musk on His PayPal Firing," Inc. 5000.
900. Robert Strauss, "The Next, Next Thing," *The Pennsylvania Gazette*, November 1, 2008, https://thepenngazette.com/the-next-next-thing/.
901. "Elon Musk on His PayPal Firing," Inc. 5000.
902. Rogan and Musk, "JRE #1609."
903. "Elon Musk," Full Send Podcast.
904. "Elon Musk," Full Send Podcast.
905. Musk, "Caltech Commencement Speech."
906. Lex Fridman and Elon Musk, "Elon Musk: Neuralink, AI, Autopilot, and the Pale Blue Dot | Lex Fridman Podcast #49," Lex Fridman, November 12, 2019, YouTube video, 36:09, https://www.youtube.com/watch?v=smK9dgdTl40.
907. Musk, "Caltech Commencement Speech."
908. Musk, "Caltech Commencement Speech."
909. Wilson and Musk, "Metaphysical Van."
910. Wilson and Musk, "Metaphysical Van."
911. "Elon Musk: 10X Every 6 Months."
912. "Elon Musk: 10X Every 6 Months."
913. Khan and Musk, "CEO of Tesla Motors and SpaceX."
914. Fridman and Musk, "Lex Fridman Podcast #252."
915. Fridman and Musk, "Lex Fridman Podcast #252."
916. "Elon Musk: Digital Superintelligence," Y Combinator.
917. *Return to Space.*
918. Musk (@elonmusk), X account.
919. "Elon Musk: 10X Every 6 Months."
920. Musk (@elonmusk), X account.
921. "Elon Musk on How to Save the Human Race," Milken Conference.
922. "Elon Musk: 10X Every 6 Months."
923. "Elon Musk: 10X Every 6 Months."
924. Musk, "Caltech Commencement Speech."
925. Fridman and Musk, "Lex Fridman Podcast #252."

926 "Elon Musk SpaceX Update at Starbase," May 2025.

927 "Elon Musk SpaceX Update, Starship Flight 3."

928 "Elon Musk at TED2022."

929 "Elon Musk SpaceX Update, Starship Flight 3."

930 "Elon Musk: 10X Every 6 Months."

931 Musk, "Caltech Commencement Speech."

932 Rogan and Musk, "JRE #1609."

933 "Elon Musk SpaceX Update at Starbase," May 2025.

934 Fridman and Musk, "Lex Fridman Podcast #438."

935 "Elon Musk SpaceX Update at Starbase," May 2025.

936 "Elon Musk SpaceX Update at Starbase," May 2025.

937 "Elon Musk SpaceX Update, Starship Flight 3."

938 "Elon Musk SpaceX Update at Starbase," May 2025.

939 "Elon Musk SpaceX Update, Starship Flight 3."

940 "Elon Musk: 10X Every 6 Months."

941 "Elon Musk SpaceX Update at Starbase," May 2025.

942 Musk and Altman, "Thinking for the Future."

943 Musk (@elonmusk), X account.

944 "Elon Musk SpaceX Update at Starbase," May 2025.

945 "Elon Musk SpaceX Update, Starship Flight 3."

946 Musk (@elonmusk), X account.

947 Fridman and Musk, "Lex Fridman Podcast #252."

948 Khan and Musk, "CEO of Tesla Motors and SpaceX."

949 Urban, "SpaceX Will Colonize Mars, Part 2."

950 "Elon Musk SpaceX Update at Starbase," May 2025.

951 "Elon Musk," Full Send Podcast.

952 "Elon Musk Answers Your Questions," SXSW 2018.

953 "Elon Musk SpaceX Update at Starbase," May 2025.

954 Rogan and Musk, "JRE #1609."

955 "Elon Musk," Full Send Podcast.

956 "Elon Musk," Full Send Podcast.

957 Rogan and Musk, "JRE #1609."

958 "Jeff Skoll Talks with Elon and Kimbal Musk."

959 "Elon Musk SpaceX Update, Starship Flight 3."

960 "Elon Musk SpaceX Update, Starship Flight 3."

961 Rogan and Musk, "JRE #1609."

962 "Elon Musk SpaceX Update, Starship Flight 3."

963 "Elon Musk at TED2022."

964 Rogan and Musk, "JRE #1609."

965 "Elon Musk," Full Send Podcast.

966 "Elon Musk's NEW EPIC Rant."

967 "Elon Musk," Full Send Podcast.

968 Musk and Altman, "Thinking for the Future."

969 "Elon Musk Answers Your Questions," SXSW 2018.

970 Tim Urban, "SpaceX's Big F***ing Rocket: The Full Story," *Wait But Why* (blog), September 29, 2016, https://waitbutwhy.com/2016/09/spacexs-big-fking-rocket-the-full-story.html.

971 "Elon Musk Answers Your Questions," SXSW 2018.

972 Rogan and Musk, "JRE #1609."

973 "Elon Musk's Vision for the Future."

974 Urban, "SpaceX's Big F***ing Rocket."

975 *Return to Space.*

976 Urban, "SpaceX's Big F***ing Rocket."

977 "Elon Musk at TED2022."

978 "Elon Musk: Digital Superintelligence," Y Combinator.

979 Urban, "SpaceX Will Colonize Mars, Part 2."

980 Urban, "SpaceX Will Colonize Mars, Part 2."

981 Rogan and Musk, "JRE #1609."

982 Musk, "Caltech Commencement Speech."

983 The Editors of Encyclopaedia Britannica, "Elon Musk," Britannica Money, *Encyclopaedia Britannica*, accessed November 13, 2025, https://www.britannica.com/biography/Elon-Musk.

984 Vance, *Elon Musk.*

985 Ashlee Vance, "Elon Musk: The College Years," *Esquire*, June 5, 2015, https://www.esquire.com/entertainment/books/a35508/elon-musk-college-years-canada-u-penn/.

986 Vance, "Elon Musk: The College Years."

987 Vance, "Elon Musk: The College Years."

988 Rogan and Musk, "JRE #1609."

989 "Jeff Skoll Talks with Elon and Kimbal Musk."

990 Mahnoor Khan, "Why Elon Musk Dropped Out of Stanford After Only Two Days," *Fortune*, February 15, 2022, https://fortune.com/2022/02/15/why-elon-musk-dropped-out-of-stanford/.

991 Vance, *Elon Musk*.

992 Vance, *Elon Musk*; Sara-Jayne Slack, "Elon Musk Facts: History, Achievements and Net Worth," Academy Center, Investing.com, last modified August 21, 2024, https://www.investing.com/academy/statistics/elon-musk-facts/.

993 Tom Huddleston Jr., "Elon Musk Slept on His Office Couch and 'Showered at the YMCA' While Starting His First Company," *CNBC*, June 19, 2018, https://www.cnbc.com/2018/06/19/how-elon-musk-founded-zip2-with-his-brother-kimbal.html.

994 "Third Row Tesla Podcast, Episode 7."

995 US Securities and Exchange Commission, "Form 10-K: PayPal, Inc.," archived August 25, 2020, https://web.archive.org/web/20200825231531/https://www.sec.gov/Archives/edgar/data/1103415/000091205702009834/a2073071z10-k405.htm.

996 Ashlee Vance, "Elon Musk's Space Dream Almost Killed Tesla," *Bloomberg*, May 14, 2015, https://www.bloomberg.com/graphics/2015-elon-musk-spacex/.

997 Vance, *Elon Musk*.

998 Matt Burns, "A Brief History of Tesla," *TechCrunch*, October 8, 2014, https://web.archive.org/web/20150717064829/https://techcrunch.com/gallery/a-brief-history-of-tesla/#/slide3.

999 "Series C: Tesla," Crunchbase, accessed November 13, 2025, https://www.crunchbase.com/funding_round/tesla-motors-series-c--ced5cae2.

1000 Berger, *Liftoff*.

1001 Drake Baer, "The Making of Tesla: Invention, Betrayal, and the Birth of the Roadster," *Business Insider*, October 31, 2014, https://www.businessinsider.com/tesla-the-origin-story-2014-10.

1002 John Boudreau, "Tesla Motors Begins Delivering Model S Electric Cars in a Silicon Valley Milestone," *The Mercury News*, June 22, 2012, https://www.mercurynews.com/2012/06/22/tesla-motors-begins-delivering-model-s-electric-cars-in-a-silicon-valley-milestone-2/.

1003 Astra Nova School, accessed November 14, 2025, https://www.astranova.org/.

1004 Mike Wall, "Wow! SpaceX Lands Orbital Rocket Successfully in Historic First," Space.com, December 21, 2015, https://www.space.com/31420-spacex-rocket-landing-success.html.

1005 Cade Metz, "Inside OpenAI, Elon Musk's Wild Plan to Set Artificial Intelligence Free," *WIRED*, April 27, 2016, https://www.wired.com/2016/04/openai-elon-musk-sam-altman-plan-to-set-artificial-intelligence-free/?utm_source=chatgpt.com.

1006 Sony Salzman et al., "Neuralink's First Brain Implant Patient Feared Device Would Have to Be Removed," *ABC News*, May 17, 2024, https://abcnews.go.com/GMA/Wellness/neuralinks-brain-implant-patient-feared-device-removed/story?id=110325322.

1007 Fred Lambert, "Tesla Model 3: Pictures of the Very First Production Unit at the Factory," Electrek, July 9, 2017, https://electrek.co/2017/07/09/tesla-model-3-production-pictures/.

1008 Fridman and Musk, "Lex Fridman Podcast #400."

1009 Jackie Wattles, "NASA, SpaceX Launch Astronauts from US Soil for the First Time in a Decade," *CNN*, May 30, 2020, https://edition.cnn.com/2020/05/30/tech/spacex-nasa-launch-astronauts-scn/index.html.

1010 Sergei Klebnikov, "Elon Musk Is Now the Richest Person in the World, Officially Surpassing Jeff Bezos," *Forbes*, last modified January 8, 2021, https://www.forbes.com/sites/sergeiklebnikov/2021/01/08/elon-musk-is-now-the-richest-person-in-the-world-officially-surpassing-jeff-bezos/?sh=13de3e433b86.

1011 Tien Le and Vanessa Romo, "Elon Musk Is Time's 2021 Person of the Year," December 13, 2021, https://www.npr.org/2021/12/13/1063792887/elon-musk-time-person-of-the-year.

1012 Elon Musk (@elonmusk), "The first human received an implant from @Neuralink yesterday and is recovering well. Initial results show promising neuron spike detection," X, January 29, 2024, https://x.com/elonmusk/status/1752098683024220632.

1013 Mike Wendling, BBC News, "Elon Musk's Starbase in Texas Will Officially Become a City," *BBC News*, May 4, 2025, https://www.bbc.com/news/articles/c39j8rj4nmmo.

1014 Matt Durot, "Elon Musk Just Became the First Person Ever Worth $500 Billion," *Forbes*, last modified October 2, 2025, https://www.forbes.com/sites/mattdurot/2025/10/01/elon-musk-just-became-the-first-person-ever-worth-500-billion/.

1015 "Tesla AI Day 2022."

1016 Krishnan and Ramamurthy, "Elon Musk Clubhouse Interview."

1017 Krishnan and Ramamurthy, "Elon Musk Clubhouse Interview."

1018 Musk (@elonmusk), X account.

1019 "Elon Musk Answers Your Questions," SXSW 2018.

1020 Musk (@elonmusk), X account.

1021 Caitlin Shamberg, "Can Elon Musk Fix the 405?," KCRW, March 19, 2013, https://www.kcrw.com/culture/articles/can-elon-musk-fix-the-405.

1022 Musk (@elonmusk), X account.

1023 Musk (@elonmusk), X account.

1024 Musk (@elonmusk), X account.

1025 Musk (@elonmusk), X account.

1026 Musk (@elonmusk), X account.

1027 Musk (@elonmusk), X account.

1028 Musk (@elonmusk), X account.

1029 Musk (@elonmusk), X account.

1030 "Will Smith Hosts Meme Review w/ Elon Musk [MEME REVIEW] #50," PewDiePie, February 22, 2019, YouTube video, 19:48, https://www.youtube.com/watch?v=zpWYQ1YtgnI&t=1024s.

1031 Musk (@elonmusk), X account.

1032 Musk (@elonmusk), X account.

1033 Musk (@elonmusk), X account.

1034 Musk (@elonmusk), X account.

1035 "Elon Musk Recommends 12 Books That Changed His Life," Farnam Street Media, *FS* (blog), 2021, https://fs.blog/elon-musk-book-recommendations/.

1036 Fridman and Musk, "Lex Fridman Podcast #438."

1037 Musk (@elonmusk), X account.

1038 Musk (@elonmusk), X account.

1039 "Elon Musk's NEW EPIC Rant."

1040 Krishnan and Ramamurthy, "Elon Musk Clubhouse Interview."

1041 Musk (@elonmusk), X account.

1042 "Birthrate Threat," WELT Documentary.

1043 Carlin and Musk, "Engineering Victory."

1044 Musk (@elonmusk), X account.

1045 Carlin and Musk, "Engineering Victory."

1046 Musk (@elonmusk), X account.

1047 Musk (@elonmusk), X account.

1048 Richard Garriott and David Fisher, *Explore/Create: My Life in Pursuit of New Frontiers, Hidden Worlds, and the Creative Spark* (William Morrow, 2017).

1049 "Elon Musk and Kevin Rose," Kevin Rose, September 7, 2012, YouTube video, 26:42, https://www.youtube.com/watch?v=L-s_3b5fRd8.

1050 Fridman and Musk, "Lex Fridman Podcast #252."

1051 Fridman and Musk, "Lex Fridman Podcast #400."

1052 Max Tegmark, *Life 3.0: Being Human in the Age of Artificial Intelligence* (Vintage Books, 2017).

1053 Musk (@elonmusk), X account.

1054 Musk (@elonmusk), X account.

1055 Musk (@elonmusk), X account.

1056 Ian Goodfellow et al., *Deep Learning* (MIT Press, 2016).

1057 Musk (@elonmusk), X account.

1058 Musk (@elonmusk), X account.

1059 Musk (@elonmusk), X account.

1060 Peter Thiel and Blake Masters, *Zero to One: Notes on Startups, or How to Build the Future* (Crown Business, 2014).

1061 Musk (@elonmusk), X account.

1062 "Elon Musk's NEW EPIC Rant."

1063 Musk (@elonmusk), X account.

www.ingramcontent.com/pod-product-compliance
Lightning Source LLC
LaVergne TN
LVHW041958060526
838200LV00019B/383/J